PUB STROLLS IN
DERBYSHIRE

Charles Wildgoose

COUNTRYSIDE BOOKS
NEWBURY BERKSHIRE

COUNTRYSIDE BOOKS
3 Catherine Road
Newbury, Berkshire

To view our complete range of books,
please visit us at
www.countrysidebooks.co.uk

ISBN 1 85306 671 0
EAN 978 1 85306 671 9

Photographs by the author
Maps by the author and redrawn by
Techniset Typesetters

Designed by Graham Whiteman

Typeset by Techniset Typesetters, Newton-le-Willows
Produced through MRM Associates Ltd., Reading
Printed in Singapore

Contents

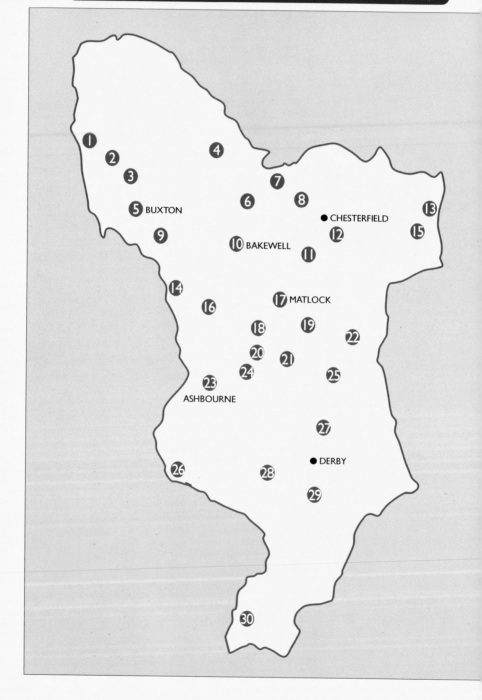

WALK

PUBLISHER'S NOTE

We hope that you obtain considerable enjoyment from this book; great care has been taken in its preparation. However, changes of landlord and actual closures are sadly not uncommon. Likewise, although at the time of publication all routes followed public rights of way or permitted paths, diversion orders can be made and permissions withdrawn.

We cannot, of course, be held responsible for such diversion orders and any inaccuracies in the text which result from these or any other changes to the routes nor any damage which might result from walkers trespassing on private property. We are anxious though that all details covering the walks and the pubs are kept up to date and would therefore welcome information from readers which would be relevant to future editions.

The sketch maps accompanying each walk are not always to scale and are intended to guide you to the starting point and give a simple but accurate idea of the route to be taken. For those who like the benefit of detailed maps, we recommend that you arm yourself with the relevant Ordnance Survey map in the Explorer or Outdoor Leisure series.

Derbyshire is a county of infinite variety and these 30 pub strolls take you from the moors in the north around Longshaw to the River Trent in the south at Swarkestone. In between you get the chance to walk underground (in Ashbourne) and to visit the village of Pentrich where the last revolution in England started. But, as they say, there is much, much more.

The circular walks range in distance from 2 to $4\frac{1}{4}$ miles and all start and finish at a good pub. For each route, you can park in the pub car park (except for Walk 1 where it is easier to park nearby). However, please remember that this is only on the understanding that you will be calling in at the pub for refreshments either before or after the walk. It is also a good idea just to let the landlord know your plans. If you do opt to leave your car on the road, please remember to park considerately with care for local residents.

These 30 circuits are classed as strolls but you would be well advised to wear boots as I can't promise you a mud and puddle free walk. And do remember that if your boots do get muddy, please leave them in the car before stepping into the pub. Very few pubs welcome walkers with dirty footwear.

Although some of the routes are flat and easy, others are a little more demanding as I'm sure you'd expect in a county such as Derbyshire. However, remember that any uphill walking is often rewarded by some superb views so it is usually well worth the extra effort.

When you've done the thirty walks I'm sure you'll agree that in this county where I live we have a very special place – one tha needs to be cherished and preserved fo future generations. Some people tend t think that the countryside never change Well, at least three walks in this book wi show that this is not so. At New Mill £500,000 has been spent building th Millennium Walkway. Even more is bein spent to extremely good effect on a faceli below Bolsover Castle. Finally, the plantin of the National Forest has started in an around Rosliston, the most southerly wal in the book. The latter is one developmen that future generations will enjoy but whic we will only see in its infancy.

As usual I have great pleasure in thankin my band of checkers: Simon and Lorrain Burnett, Frank Ogden, Ian Swindell, Phili Carter, Joe Clarke, Val Gosney, Andrev Cooke, Gary Wigley, Darren Crownshav Ruth Rhodes, Amanda Wardman, Brian an Audrey Hoon, Malcolm and Sue Fordyce Angela Waite, Anne Wiles, Carol Morri Roger Busby, Alex Mastin, Leah Travis an Jo Johnston. And I mustn't forget Harvey th Dog who by all accounts followed on particular route better than the thre ladies he was with. Thanks also to Howar Martin and Frank Groom for last minut advice – much appreciated.

Finally I would like to record my heartfe thanks to Balkees. For a fifth time I hav tried her patience by asking her to chec over a third of the walks, and she didn't le me down.

Enjoy the walks.

Charles Wildgoo.

New Mills
The Royal Oak

MAP REF: OS OUTDOOR LEISURE 1
(GR 002854)

WALK 1

DISTANCE: 4$\frac{1}{4}$ MILES

DIRECTIONS TO START: FROM THE A6 FOLLOW THE A6015 NORTH-EASTWARDS INTO NEW MILLS. BEYOND THE TRAFFIC LIGHTS TURN LEFT INTO HYDE BANK ROAD (SIGNED 'LEISURE CENTRE'). **PARKING:** PARK NEAR KINGDOM HALL.

A glance at the OS map will give no idea of the hidden delights of the Torrs Riverside Park. Indeed, you could walk along the street in New Mills and be oblivious to the gorge nearby where the rivers Sett and Goyt combine their waters. New Mills was originally a number of small villages which were renamed collectively after the new mills that had been built. In future its name is likely to be synonymous with the spectacular Millennium Walkway which is featured towards the end of the walk. Built at a cost of £525,000 and opened in early 2000 it is a stunning feature below the town centre. Whoever conceived the idea of building this deserves great credit. This fascinating walk follows three watercourses: the rivers Goyt and Sett as well as the Peak Forest Canal.

7

The Royal Oak

To find the Royal Oak, return to the A6015. Turn right and right again into Union Street, proceed to the roundabout and turn right to the pub; there is a small car park to the rear.

The Royal Oak in the centre of New Mills is a very popular family pub, favoured by locals though everyone is welcome. The present landlady has been there for a quarter of a century so she obviously likes the place and vice versa. What better testimony can you have? The food is tasty and extremely good value. There is certainly plenty of choice, from snacks to main meals and they're all homemade. So you could try steak and kidney pie, cheese and onion pie or a special such as beef stew and dumplings. There are also soups and toasties and they now provide a range of sweets such as apple pie, syrup sponge and custard or caramel apple granny. The beer is Robinson's Bitter and Hatter's Mild. Alternatively Strongbow cider is available as well as lager of course. So, after an excellent walk why not visit the Royal Oak? Children are allowed but dogs can only go in the games room. It's open weekdays from 11.30 am until 11 pm; on Saturday from 11 am to 11 pm; and on Sundays from noon until 10.30 pm – and food is now available on Sunday. Telephone: 01663 743675.

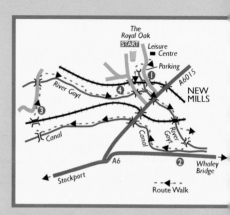

The Walk

① Keep on Hyde Bank Road to the Leisure Centre. Turn right, then right again under the road bridge just crossed. In 30 yards turn left into Torrs Riverside Park. (Remember this next section as you return this way!) With the river on your left continue towards the point where the rivers Goyt and Sett meet. Cross the wooden Millward Memorial Bridge. Pass under a two-tier bridge. Stay beside the river. After passing under another bridge ignore any path to the left. Continue along a track to Goytside Farm. Turn right immediately beyond it. Cross the Goyt. Proceed uphill on the gravel path. Turn right alongside the Peak Forest Canal.

② Stay beside this for $1\frac{1}{4}$ miles. Initially this is a lovely, rural area. Slowly New Mills becomes more evident. Pass the Marina before passing under the A6015. Open fields appear again. At the next

PLACES OF INTEREST NEARBY

New Mills Heritage and Information Centre tells the story of New Mills. From just outside the entrance there is a viewpoint down into the Torrs Riverside Park. This gives a spectacular view of the Millennium Walkway and the ruined mill. Telephone: 01663 746904.

The Millennium Walkway in New Mills

ridge bear right up the side of it (not
nder it). Turn right down the track
Lower Greenshall Lane) alongside a
wood on your left.

3) At the bottom continue forward
ignoring the road zigzagging uphill to the
left. Cross the Goyt by a road-bridge. In
00 yards turn right into Torrs Riverside
Park again. Stay on the path (following the
GW' and Midshires Way waymarks)
keeping right with the river on your
ight. Pass a guidepost, the Ridgeway is
just 210 miles away! After climbing a stile
beside a gate bear half-left (ignoring the
track ahead and the path to the left) to
follow the 'GW' and Midshires Way
waymarks on a gravel path through a
wood. Turn right beyond a converted

stone building. Turn left before reaching
a pair of redbrick houses on the right to
enter an area of parkland. Follow the path
to the far side. When you reach the end of
a road (beside some factory buildings)
take the path running along the right side
of it. This descends to the right and away
from the road.

4) You reach the impressive Torrs
Millennium Walkway which cost
£525,000. Cross this spectacular
construction. Keep forward with the
river on your right. Pass some ruined
buildings on your right too. Stay beside
the river to reach the steps which you
descended into the riverside park. Climb
them and retrace your route back to your
car.

Buxworth
The Navigation Inn

MAP REF: OS OUTDOOR LEISURE 1
(GR 023821)

WALK 2

DISTANCE: $2^3/_4$ MILES

DIRECTIONS TO START: HEAD NORTH ON THE A6 FOR 400 YARDS FROM THE WHALEY
BRIDGE ROUNDABOUT. THEN FORK RIGHT ON THE B6062. A MILE LATER, IN FRONT
OF BUXWORTH PRIMARY SCHOOL, TURN SHARP RIGHT DOWN TO THE NAVIGATION INN.
PARKING: PARK ON THE FAR SIDE OF THE INN BETWEEN IT AND BUGSWORTH BASIN.

Buxworth was called 'Bugsworth' until early in the 20th century. Did it change its name because some locals didn't fancy the connection with 'bugs'? The original name is fortunately retained with the Bugsworth Basin which lies on the opposite side of the car park from the Navigation Inn. The Basin marks the end of the Peak Forest Canal and it is a fitting conclusion to a walk, nearly half of which runs alongside the canal. Look out as you walk for the information panels which will supply you with further information as regards the history of the canal. Initially the walk rises away from Buxworth through the fields to the north-west of the village. It is the final section though which is the greatest delight – a mile of gentle walking alongside the canal, while the world bustles along the A6 nearby. Take your time – admire the scenery, the wildlife and look out for narrow boats.

The Navigation Inn

Lovers of *Coronation Street* will be particularly interested in this inn as Pat Phoenix who played Elsie Tanner used to own it. There's much, much more to it though. For instance, the last person to be hanged in Derby Jail was John Cotton, a local boatman. He was 70 when he murdered his young wife on a boat moored in Bugsworth Basin. The full story (plus old photographs of Bugsworth Basin) is in the snug. The food is excellent with specials like Cheshire pork with apple sauce, crackling and apricot and pine nut stuffing or chicken and penne pasta. There's a snack menu too including a tuna melt and a 4oz rump steak with onions. As you can see, something with a bit of a difference. Children and dogs are welcome but our canine friends have to stay away from all eating areas I'm afraid. As regards beer the regulars are Timothy Taylor Landlord, Webster's Yorkshire Bitter and Marston's Pedigree. Then there are guests such as Abbot Ale and for those who prefer their cider, Strongbow is always on sale. During the summer they also have some guest ciders. This is an all-day pub and it is full of interest – you have to visit it to see what I mean.

Telephone: 01663 732072.

The pub also has an award winning website – www.navigationinn.co.uk

The Walk

① From the car park between the inn and Bugsworth Basin return to the B6062. Turn right (for Chinley). Pass under the railway bridge. Turn left on the cobbled track immediately after house number 9. Follow the footpath through the farmyard of Knowltop passing a converted barn on the right climbing stiles by two farm gates beyond. Enter the field and walk on the grassy track with a wall on your left.

② In the second field keep forward with the electricity pylons on your left. Pass through the right-hand of two gateways and enter a third field, keeping the pylons on your left. Cross a stile into the fourth field. Head towards the pylon directly ahead. 50 or 60 yards before you reach it, cross the stone step-stile almost immediately below the cables. Walk alongside the wall on your left beyond to enter another field with the wall now on your right (and the electricity cables above!). Towards the end of this field pass under the electricity lines to reach a stile. Follow the fenced path then climb a stile, continuing downhill to walk to the lowest part of the field with the railway line just a few yards to your left. (The pylons are now away to your right.)

③ Pass through a stile, cross a small

PLACES OF INTEREST NEARBY

To the west of Buxworth is **Lyme Park**, a National Trust property set in an ancient deer park well worth exploring. The house was the setting for 'Pemberley' in the BBC's adaptation of Jane Austen's *Pride and Prejudice*. For further details telephone 01663 762023.

Teapot Cottages beside the Peak Forest Canal

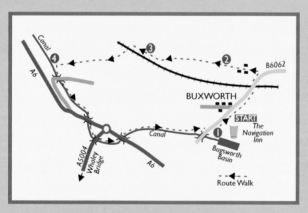

second one passes between the stream on your left and an attractive house on the right. Follow the track at the bottom of this second property to cross the River Goyt. Beyond this pass the sewage works to reach the Peak Forest Canal.

④ It's nearly all plain sailing now! Turn left alongside the canal (keeping the canal on your right) for the next $1^1/_4$ miles to reach the Navigation Inn. As you go ignore the canal spur off to the right to Whaley Bridge and look out for the information panels relating to Bugsworth Basin.

stream and proceed along the walled path in front for 175 yards. Turn left at a track to pass under two railway bridges. Follow the stony track downhill passing a couple of properties. The path through the

Combs
The Beehive Inn

| MAP REF: OS OUTDOOR LEISURE 24 (GR 041786) | WALK 3 | DISTANCE: 3½ MILES |

DIRECTIONS TO START: FROM THE B5740 WHALEY BRIDGE TO CHAPEL-EN-LE-FRITH ROAD HEAD SOUTH FOR A MILE TO REACH COMBS. **PARKING:** THE BEEHIVE CAR PARK IS ON THE LEFT JUST BEFORE YOU REACH THE PUB ON THE RIGHT.

To my shame I had never visited Combs before I started writing this book. Perhaps it has something to do with the fact that on the OS map it is almost submerged by the broad, green, National Park boundary. It's on a fold in the map too. All factors which can discourage exploration! But now ... well, what a 'discovery'. Set in the valley below Combs Edge this village is a little gem. Surrounded by high ground with just the one pub, Combs is lovely. The route involves a climb from valley bottom to mountain high (well, almost) but take your time and savour the walk. The views from the higher ground are far reaching and to be enjoyed. There's also a crib-hole to look out for on the walk. This is a hole built in a wall for the sheep to pass through from one field to another. There is one peculiarity though – the reservoir nearby is sometimes spelt 'Coombs' not 'Combs'.

The Beehive Inn

Absolutely everything is home-made at the Beehive Inn. This is an attractive pub in a lovely village. It was originally two buildings – a farmhouse with a pub grafted on the front, and the farmhouse itself had a licence to sell beer. So for as long as anyone can remember there's been beer available at these premises. In the summertime the benches outside are ideal to enjoy the summer sunshine. Black Sheep plus one guest (often Bass) is available for those who want a glass of beer, or Strongbow if you prefer cider. There's plenty of choice at the Beehive where they serve 'fresh food, not fast food' and they add 'thanks for being patient at busy times.' So what have they got to offer? Well, there's main courses such as homemade steak and ale pie, fresh-made vegetable stroganoff and gammon steak with egg or pineapple. If you fancy a bit on the side, there's chipped, mashed or new potatoes, vegetables or onion rings. You could perhaps round off with a dessert such as warm banoffee pie and cream or chocolate brownie cheesecake. Children are welcome but dogs are restricted to the taproom. The pub opens from noon until 3 pm and 6 pm until 11 pm during the week but all day at the weekend. Telephone: 01298 812758.

The Walk

① Facing the front of the Beehive, take the road to the left of it, forking left almost immediately. Turn left at Quietways. Ascend this tree-lined lane

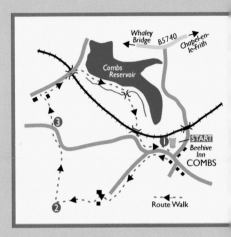

beside a tiny brook. It may say it's a private road, but this lane is also a public footpath! Pass Haylee, with views to the left of Combs Edge. At Haylee Farm stay on the track bearing uphill round to the right towards a farmhouse, then left in front of it. Turn right through the gate immediately past the water troughs. Follow the rough track ahead alongside a wall, then across the field. Views open up on the right including Combs Reservoir. Pass the crib-hole in the wall on the right. Stay on the track beside the wall again to zigzag through a marshy area before passing through a gateway.

② Turn right onto a gravel track. Proceed alongside a wall on your right, descending with a TV mast uphill to your left. There are good views of Castle

PLACES OF INTEREST NEARBY

Buxton Museum (telephone: 01298 24658) is one possibility, telling the story of the area, and then there's also Poole's Cavern, with its fascinating rock formations. They can be contacted on 01298 26978. If you'd like to explore underground then this will be of great interest to you.

...erlooking Coombs reservoir

...aze including the embankments of the ...cient hill fort. Descend to pass ...rough a farm gate. Continue down ...e tarmac driveway towards the ...servoir. Pass Thornylee Farm on the ...ght. At another tarmac lane rising from ...e right, turn left up the stony track. ...ss under some beech trees. In 120 ...rds (with the TV mast to your left) ...imb the stone stile over the wall.

...) Bear slightly left down the 'holloway' ... the field bottom. Keeping the wall on ...ur right subsequently cross a stile and ...ep forward (descending as you go). Pass ...rough two gates to reach the drive of ...nstead Farm. Walk forward for a few yards, pass through a gate and turn sharp right down the driveway towards the reservoir. Cross two bridges. Turn right keeping Combs Reservoir on your left and Meveril Brook to your right. Stay beside the brook and half a mile later bear right over a footbridge. Walk across the corner of the field. Pass through a gap at the base of an oak tree. Bear half-left, walking diagonally across the field to the far corner to a stile underneath a holly bush. Beyond this bear half-right to pass under the railway bridge at the top of the field. (This section of path before the railway bridge can be very boggy and wet after wet weather so be aware!) Walk forward to the lane beyond. Turn left back to Combs.

Hope
The Woodroffe Arms Hotel

MAP REF: OS OUTDOOR LEISURE 1 (GR 172835)	**WALK 4**	DISTANCE: 3 MILES

DIRECTIONS TO START: THE WOODROFFE ARMS HOTEL IS ON THE A625 IN THE MIDDLE OF HOPE. IT IS ON THE LEFT IF YOU ARE HEADING WEST. **PARKING:** USE THE PUB CAR PARK. THERE IS A PUBLIC CAR PARK NEXT TO IT IF YOU PREFER.

One mile to the north of Hope lie Win Hill and Lose (pronounced 'Loose') Hill. It is believed that over 1,000 years ago a battle was fought hereabouts with the winners camping on Win Hill and the losers … yes, you've got it. Surely there must be some truth in this legend? Back to what we know to be fact. The historical connection continues on the walk as we step even further back in time, walking directly over all that remains of the Roman fort of Navio. You may no realise the remains are there but they are After you've walked across the particula field look out for the information board o the far side. You also pass a pinfold as yo go – just over the bridge at the start of th walk – where stray animals were kep Today you may well have a feeling o being in real walking country, which o course you are. Just 3 miles away is th start of the Pennine Way.

The Woodroffe Arms Hotel

The hotel is 400 years old though the catering and everything about the pub is definitely up to date. There's a warm welcome here too. There is a very good local trade which is a sign that the Woodroffe Arms has got it right. It has a good reputation for food and drink. The beers are Timothy Taylor Landlord, Bass and John Smith Cask. Strongbow cider is also on tap. Children are welcome and guide dogs. Other dogs can be let in when food is not being served. The food is good value, with lots of choice ranging from toasted sandwiches, baguettes, jacket potatoes, omelettes and burgers to chicken curry, pork loin poached in milk, spicy pork casserole and lamb shank! There's also a children's menu including chicken nuggets and fish-o-saurus. You could enjoy these dishes in their nice dining conservatory. Like so many pubs now (especially in the Peak District) the Woodroffe Arms is open all day from noon until 11 pm (except Sundays when it's noon until 10.30 pm). Telephone: 01433 620351.

The Walk

① Walk down Pindale Road beside the pub. Cross the bridge (with a pinfold beyond) and 100 yards later ascend Eccles Lane. To the left is Win Hill. After 175 yards climb a stile on the left. Follow the track across the field ahead. In the second field keep forward alongside woodland on the right. The view opens out. Stay beside the trees, crossing a number of stiles. Continue alongside the trees to cross a footbridge.

② Keep forward alongside the fence beyond. Continue in this direction across the open field. This contains the remains of Navio, a Roman fort dating to the third century AD. In the last field before the road bear slightly right to the road.

③ Turn left for 300 yards crossing Bradwell Brook and the River Noe. Beyond the road bridge take the stile on the left. Follow the direction of the signpost towards the clump of trees projecting into the field. Continue in this direction to a stile 30 yards from the stone outbuilding at the far end of the field. Turn left on the road passing a cottage on the right. Beyond the wood behind the cottage turn right. Walk up the right side of the field. Stay beside the small brook along a fenced path to reach a track.

④ Turn left. At the end of the terraced cottages turn right. Cross the bridge over the railway line. Bear right beyond, then left to walk up the right side of the field ahead towards Win Hill.

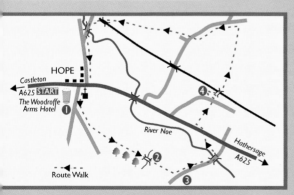

The village of Hope

Keep in the same direction through a number of fields, ignoring a cross path at one point. Turn left down a tarmac lane. Ignore two driveways to the right. Pass Crabtree Meadow on your left. Turn right on the drive to Farfield Farm and 100 yards later keep left of a pair of dressed stone gateposts, continuing down a track. Stay on the track beside a hedge (ignoring a gate on your left). Enter the trees beyond. Pass under a railway bridge, then pass the cemetery on your right. Subsequently bear left at the lane. Stay on this to cross a bridge to the road. Turn left back to Hope.

PLACES OF INTEREST NEARBY

Castleton is a mile to the west and there you have the choice of four caverns to visit. They are (in no particular order) Speedwell Cavern (telephone: 01433 620512), Blue John Cavern (telephone: 01433 620638), Peak Cavern (telephone: 01433 620285) and Treak Cliff Cavern (telephone: 01433 620571). I'm not suggesting you go down them all in one afternoon.

Buxton
The Old Sun Inn

MAP REF: OS OUTDOOR LEISURE 24 (GR 058730)

WALK 5

DISTANCE: 2¹⁄₂ MILES

DIRECTIONS TO START: HEAD NORTH-WESTWARDS ON THE A515 INTO BUXTON. AT THE TRAFFIC LIGHTS KEEP FORWARD TOWARDS THE TOWN CENTRE. THE OLD SUN INN IS A LITTLE FURTHER ALONG ON THE RIGHT. **PARKING:** THE PUB HAS ONLY A VERY SMALL CAR PARK. USE PUBLIC CAR PARKS NEARBY I.E. THE MARKET PLACE, THOUGH MARKETS ARE HELD TUESDAYS AND SATURDAYS.

This is a walk of two halves in the popular spa town of Buxton. First a steady ascent, then a steady descent. The first half of the walk sees you rising up to Solomon's Temple overlooking Buxton. Look around as there are some fine views. Once at the top a last, steep, climb will take you up to the top of the Temple. From here you can see even more of the surrounding countryside – or perhaps just your friends or family resting on the ground below this folly! On the way back at least you'll know it's all downhill (well, very nearly). Initially you descend through Grinlow Wood to the car park by Poole's Cavern. Try and visit this after your meal if you have time. Then there is a lovely section through the Pavilion Gardens past the elegant houses built overlooking this parkland.

The Old Sun Inn

From the outside perhaps the Old Sun Inn looks like many other 'town' pubs and I'm sure you'll be pleased to see stabling is still available! Inside though you'll be in for a real surprise. It's full of character and charm – a real pub. As the landlord says, it's 'very olde worlde with lots of nooks and crannies'. Part of the pub dates back to the 16th century with Guinness being bottled here in the past under licence in the cellars. Some of the original bottles are still on view. The food is set out on a comprehensive and interesting menu with some specials on a blackboard. For starters there are items like hot king prawns with limes and chilli mayonnaise. The main courses comprise dishes such as chicken Wensleydale, old English fish pie and Canadian melt. The sandwiches are interesting too with the Chicken BBQ melt sounding tasty. As regards beers, they are cask conditioned, and you can choose from three regulars (Marston's Bitter, Pedigree and Bank's Bitter) and three guests which could include Marston's Old Empire, Smile's Slap and Tipple and Hopback's Summer Lightning. If you're a cider lover then Scrumpy Jack is available. Well behaved children are allowed but no dogs. The pub is open Monday to Saturday from 11.30 am to 11 pm; and Sundays from midday to 10.30 pm. Food is available from a wide menu from 12 noon until 2.30 pm and 6.30 pm until 10 pm in the week and from midday until 4 pm at weekends. Telephone: 01298 23452.

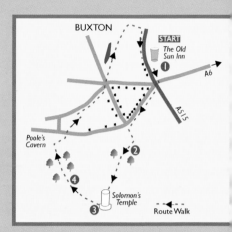

The Walk

① With your back to the inn turn left downhill to the traffic lights. Cross to Green Lane (between London Road and West Road) and leave behind the hustle and bustle. With College Road on the right, turn left along the gravel path. After 120 yards turn right through a stone gap stile. Cross the playing fields ahead. Follow the obvious path up the grassy bank into the trees.

② Follow the path bearing right into the trees. Bear left uphill after 70 yards where it forks to reach some fields. Keep forward up the short steep slope. Solomon's Temple lies ahead. Walk straight towards it. (If it's foggy just keep walking forward.)

PLACES OF INTEREST NEARBY

Buxton Museum (telephone: 01298 24658) is one possibility and Poole's Cavern (telephone: 01298 26978) another. You'll pass the entrance to the latter on the walk. The Pavilion Gardens are worth exploring and the buildings in the vicinity of the Opera House.

Solomon's Temple

③ With your back to the Tower (looking back the way you've just come) walk left. Head downhill towards the far end of the wood on the right. As you progress, the stile you're aiming for should become obvious. Just before the stile pass through a pair of redundant gateposts. Climb the stile into Grinlow Wood (ignore the gravel path leading to some steps).

④ Follow the track through the wood (ignore another to the right after 100 yards). Keep on the main track ignoring all others. Follow the waymarks for Poole's Cavern. Descend some steps to the right into the Poole's Cavern car park. Walk directly forward across this to a gate (between a house and a stone building)

with a walled path beyond. Continue along this path to the road. Cross this and turn left for 20 yards. Turn right on the walled path. When it reaches a road turn right to reach a large crossroads with Macclesfield Road to the left. Cross straight over. Proceed along the wide gravel path (between Burlington Road and Bath Road) into the Pavilion Gardens. On the right are the impressive houses and hotels overlooking the Gardens. At Derby House Nursing Home turn right up the road (Fountain Street). Keep forward at the crossroads (still on Fountain Street). Then cross another road before reaching the market place. Walk forward to the main street and turn right back to the inn.

Eyam
The Miners Arms

MAP REF: OS OUTDOOR LEISURE 24 (GR 219765)	WALK 6	DISTANCE: 2¼ MILES

DIRECTIONS TO START: FROM THE A623 TAKE THE B6521 HEADING NORTH INTO EYAM. IN THE CENTRE OF THE VILLAGE BEAR LEFT INTO WATER LANE. THE PUB IS VISIBLE AHEAD.
PARKING: IN THE PUB CAR PARK, THIS IS JUST BEYOND THE PUB AND BEHIND IT.

Eyam (pronounced 'eem') is best known not just for the decimation of its population in the mid-17th century but for the resilience of its residents in cutting themselves off from the outside world to try and stop the bubonic plague from spreading to surrounding villages. The walk takes due note of this, passing or visiting a number of relevant sites. There's a stiffish climb initially to reach Mompesson's Well.

William Mompesson was the local minister and he led the villagers in their efforts to stop the plague from spreading. Mompesson's Well was one of the places where neighbouring villagers left food and medicines for the residents of Eyam to collect. Later the route descends The Nook and then Hawkhill Road until you reach Eyam Museum. The rest of the walk passes through the village past the Hall, the Sheep Roast and the Plague Cottages.

The Miners Arms

This 17th century inn, built in 1630, is another pub that is a bit of a surprise when you get inside it. It has quite a history having a pair of ghosts, Sarah and Emily, who apparently died in a fire on the site before the pub was built. Then there's the story of the Reverend Hunt who in 1684 got himself into a bit of a pickle by getting married, whilst he was drunk, to the then landlord's daughter.

There is plenty to choose from foodwise. At lunchtime the bar food comprises dishes such as light and crispy filled baguettes, ploughman's lunch, soup, braised beef in stout sauce and crispy roast duck. Sunday lunch comprises a roast with a choice of four meats: turkey, lamb cutlets, beef and pork. During the evening restaurant food only is served. The pub is open on Monday from 7 pm to 11 pm only but no food is served on this night. On Tuesday through to Saturday it is open from 12 noon until 3 pm (with food from 12 noon until 2 pm) and from 7 pm until 11 pm (food available from 7 pm to 9 pm). On Sunday it is open from 12 noon to 10.30 pm but food is only available from noon until 2 pm. So remember there is no food on Monday and Sunday evenings. The beer that is available is London Pride, Stones and Worthingtons. There is only bottled cider, namely Red C and Dry Blackthorn. Finally, children are welcome and dogs too, though only in the bar when food is not being served. Telephone: 01433 630853.

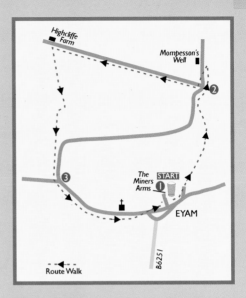

The Walk

① With your back to the pub entrance turn left along Water Lane, then left again beside the butchers. Proceed along the road passing Miners Arms Croft and the Wesleyan Reform church. After this turn left into Riley Back Lane and follow it round to the right after 10 yards. This tarmac access road leads uphill before downgrading to a path leading along the edge of a wood. Where the path splits take the right fork uphill and ascend the wide stony path. This is a lovely path under broad-leaved trees though it changes character under some conifers. At the top of the plantation keep on the path.

PLACES OF INTEREST NEARBY

There's **Eyam Museum** (telephone: 01433 631371 or out of opening hours 01433 630777) where you can learn about the plague. Alternatively visit **Eyam Hall** (telephone: 01433 631976), an interesting house with craft centre attached. Try and buy a copy of the Eyam Map (published 2000). This will tell you even more about the village.

23

Hall Hill Troughs

The path forks again – take the lower route. This starts to lead uphill until you're walking along the top of the wood. Bear right up to the road.

② Turn right for 75 yards then left along the Bretton road. Before you take the Bretton road though, walk uphill for 100 yards to visit Mompesson's Well. Food was brought here by neighbouring villagers during the plague in the mid 17th century. Return to the Bretton road. Follow this for $^{1}/_{2}$ mile passing the chimney of Ladywash Mine on the right. Continue to Highcliffe Farm and Highcliffe Barns. Turn sharp left here and descend the track until it becomes a tarmac access road. Stay on this to reach the corner of a road.

Continue downhill to pass Eyam Museum on the right. Beyond that pass Hall Hill Troughs – an early example of a public water supply.

③ At the bottom of the hill – 30 yards beyond the troughs – turn left into the main street. Pass Eyam Hall on the left and some stocks on the right. Then pass the Sheep Roast and immediately afterwards Rose Cottage where members of the Thorpe family died during the plague. Then pass Plague Cottage where the first victim died. Once past the church the road will bring you back into the centre of the village. Turn left at Water Lane back to the pub.

Longshaw
The Grouse Inn

DIRECTIONS TO START: FROM THE TRAFFIC LIGHTS AT CALVER CROSSROADS TAKE THE B6001 HEADING NORTH. AFTER 350 YARDS FORK RIGHT ONTO THE B6054. STAY ON THIS FOR $2^1/_2$ MILES CLIMBING STEADILY TO REACH THE GROUSE INN ON THE LEFT. **PARKING:** WALKERS CAN USE THE PUB CAR PARK. THERE IS A SMALL LAY-BY JUST DOWN THE ROAD WHICH YOU MAY PREFER.

This is a walk which is about a mile from the nearest village, though the centre of Sheffield is less than eight miles away. The boundary with South Yorkshire is even nearer. Still, this is Derbyshire and long may it remain so. The walk is a beauty but without anything too strenuous. The distant views towards Win Hill, Lose Hill and Kinder Scout are to be savoured with, nearer to hand, Carl Wark and Higger Tor impressive as you look right when you reach the driveway leading into Longshaw Lodge. The Lodge was a hunting lodge, now owned by the National Trust. There are toilets and a tea room here for those who might fancy taking the walk at a leisurely pace. The scenery is truly wonderful and there are a number of places where you can sit down and consider your lot. A walk to be savoured at any time of the year although, be warned, it can be a bit 'fresh' on the outward route if there's a cool wind.

The Grouse Inn

The Grouse Inn stands alone on the moors overlooking the Derwent valley. It provides a welcome respite from those cool days you can often get up in the north of Derbyshire. There's a welcome for everyone as there's good food and beer to be had here. The beers are Bank's Bitter, Marston's Pedigree and Deuchar's and there's usually a guest available too. Strongbow cider is also sold. The food is very tasty, the home-made steak pie being excellent. Then there are other dishes like cod, king prawns and garlic, turmeric chicken and wholetail Whitby scampi which are just as popular. One thing that may prove popular is the large selection of malt whiskies – over 40.

Although parts of the pub are over 300 years old there isn't a ghost. Perhaps this has something to do with the fact that during the last 200 years there have only been two families resident here. As regards opening during the week, it's noon until 3 pm and 6 pm until 11 pm. Then at weekends it's noon until 11 pm on Saturday and noon until 10.30 pm on Sunday. Food is available every lunchtime from noon until 2.30 pm and every evening (except Monday) from 7 pm until 9.30 pm. Telephone: 01433 630423.

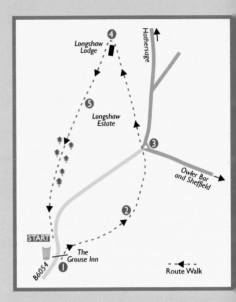

The Walk

① From the Grouse turn left up the B6054 for 40 yards. Pass through the bridlegate on the right. Cross the field (keeping the marshy area to your right) towards another bridlegate. Follow the bridleway to enter the Eastern Moors Estate. Pass through some silver birches. Where the path splits at the base of some boulders turn left. Follow the grassy bridleway slightly uphill. The view on the left opens out with Eyam Moor surmounted by a transmitter. To the right of this are Lose Hill and Win Hill with Kinder Scout beyond. Pass through a bridlegate onto White Edge Moor, part of the Longshaw Estate.

② Stay on the bridleway as it rises and bears right round a hillock. It then straightens out. Continue past White

PLACES OF INTEREST NEARBY

Chatsworth House (telephone: 01246 582204) is a few miles to the south. Besides the house there's the Farm and the Gardens. Probably more than enough to occupy you for an afternoon. The Old House Museum (no telephone number) in Bakewell is also an interesting way of passing an hour or so.

Higger Tor from the Longshaw Estate

Lodge Lodge to your left. As you proceed look out for the distinctive flat top of Higger Tor to your left with Carl Wark (an ancient hillfort) in front of it. Before long the bridleway joins the gravel driveway to the lodge. Walk on this in the same direction as before.

3 At the road, cross to the grass triangle carefully. Keep forward to the gate gaining access to the area known as Wooden Pole. The pole would have been a marker for travellers in days gone by. Follow the wide grassy path descending gently to the left of the pole. Ignore another path coming in sharply from the left. Continue to a gate with beech trees beyond. Enter this wood to walk behind the buildings of Longshaw Lodge. Ignore all other paths until you bend round to the left to reach the access road to the Lodge.

④ Cross the driveway, descend some steps and turn left in front of the Lodge. After passing through a small gate you stand under five yew trees. Avoid the path descending gently to the right, proceed forward through another small gate and keep on the track ahead.

⑤ Stay on this track. Keep forward where another crosses it. The track brings you back to the B6054. Turn right back to the pub.

Millthorpe
The Royal Oak

MAP REF: OS OUTDOOR LEISURE 24 (GR 317764)   **WALK 8**   **DISTANCE:** 2 MILES

DIRECTIONS TO START: FROM THE OWLER BAR ROUNDABOUT SOUTH OF SHEFFIELD FOLLOW THE B6051 SOUTH-EASTWARDS FOR A COUPLE OF MILES. THE ROYAL OAK IS ON THE LEFT.
PARKING: FEEL FREE TO PARK IN THE PUB CAR PARK BUT LET THE LANDLORD KNOW FIRST PLEASE.

This is a lovely rural stroll that 'kisses' the Peak Park boundary for 150 yards. The rest of it is outside the boundary. When the National Park was created over 50 years ago Millthorpe and its environs could just as easily have been in the Park as outside it – such is its beautiful setting. After leaving the Royal Oak one of the first features you'll encounter is the ford. This is a timeless spot. You could be back at the beginning of the last century instead of at the beginning of this one. Incidentally, if you get the chance have a closer look at the OS White Peak map. There are some delightful place-names round here: Johnnygate, Dobmeadow Wood, Highlightley Lane and Rumbling Street. Names which typify the wonderful variety of the English countryside and all within a mile of Millthorpe.

The Royal Oak

Parts of the Royal Oak date back to 1650, becoming an alehouse in 1840. Long may it continue. One of its more unusual claims to fame is that it once gave shelter to a Shetland pony which was freezing cold. Perhaps they should have given it some of the Rocket Fuel they sell. 'Rocket fuel' (or just 'rocket') is what they call the Carling Export round here. The landlord reckons it's the best kept lager around. You must try it. If you're a beer-lover though don't worry, you can try the Wards or John Smith's, or their guest ale (Greene King IPA at time of writing); or if you prefer cider, Taunton's Dry Blackthorn. The food is genuinely home-made with no frozen food used. The menu changes but the sort of dishes you can expect to sample are chilli con carne, cottage pie, lasagne, toasted cheese, plus ploughman's and sweets such as treacle tarts and fruit crumbles.

Opening times are Sundays from midday until 4 pm, Tuesdays to Fridays from 5.30 pm until 11 pm, and Saturdays from 12 noon until 3 pm and 5.30 pm until 11 pm. If the weather is good then try the large beer garden. This is in fact the only place where children can go as there is a bar in each room of the pub. As regards dogs they can only go into the pub when food is not being served. Telephone: 0114 2890870.

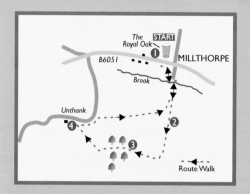

The Walk

① With your back to the pub turn left along the lane. Turn right at the crossroads down Mill Lane. Cross the ford over Millthorpe Brook. Continue along the track ignoring a path on your right. At the entrance to Mill Farm climb the stile, resisting the temptation to follow the hedged path ahead. Walk along the left side of the field beyond. Head half-right across the second field. Cross a footbridge over Pingle Dike. Almost immediately climb a stile. Bear right to cross another a few yards beyond.

② Though you may be tempted to proceed alongside the wooded area on your right, turn left walking slightly uphill alongside the hedge on your left. Pass through into the next field with the hedge now on your right. In 60 yards before the

PLACES OF INTEREST NEARBY

Chatsworth House and gardens (telephone: 01246 582204) is a fascinating place to visit. Then to the west is **The Revolution House** (telephone: 01246 453554) in Old Whittington, a village just north of Chesterfield. A visit to Chesterfield itself with its Crooked Spire is also worth considering.

The ford at Millthorpe

end of the field turn right through the gateway. Walk towards the wood ahead beside a hedge on your left. In the field in front of Rose Wood bear slightly left into the trees.

③ Follow the main path into the wood. Ignore all side paths. The path eventually bears left over a plank footbridge before gently rising to the edge of the wood. Leave the wood (having crossed another path running parallel to the edge of it). Head directly across the field to walk along the track running along the left side of the hedge leading away from you. Pass through a stile at the far end of the hedge. Cross to a squeezer stile (to the right of a bungalow) across the field.

④ Turn right at the lane beyond. Follow this for 120 yards as it bears right passing handful of properties. Where the road bends left keep forward through the stil noting that the right-hand stoop appears t be an old stone roller spliced in hal Proceed along the right side of the first tw fields ahead. (The walked line in the firs field is on the left side of the hedge. Th definitive footpath is actually on the othe side and not walkable at present! If th situation changes, then presumably th definitive path will be waymarked and yo should follow the waymarks.) Cross a stil onto a lawned area. Walk forward keepin to the left of the house. Continue alon the sunken lane back to the track you use earlier. Turn left back to the start.

Chelmorton
The Church Inn

MAP REF: OS OUTDOOR LEISURE 24
(GR 115703)

WALK 9

DISTANCE: $2^3/_4$ MILES

DIRECTIONS TO START: 1¼ MILES PAST THE TADDINGTON BYPASS ON THE A6 TURN LEFT ON THE A5270. LOOK OUT FOR THE SIGNS FOR CHELMORTON ON THE LEFT. THE PUB IS AT THE HIGHEST POINT OF THE VILLAGE BY THE CHURCH. **PARKING:** PARK (CAREFULLY AND CONSIDERATELY) NEAR THE PUB OR LOWER DOWN ON THE VILLAGE STREET. THERE IS NO PUB CAR PARK.

Someone described this walk as being 'all grass'. To be fair, it's a bit more than that. For instance, look at the 1:25 000 OS map covering Chelmorton and one thing will be immediately obvious – the way the strip-like fields run at right angles to this one-street village. The fields have been described as one of the best examples of their type in this country, if not the best. And any village that has a spring which rejoices in the name of Illy Willy Water must have

something going for it. The spring is just up the road from the pub if you want to say you've seen it. The weathervane on the church spire is rather grand too. This is a gilded locust, the symbol of St John the Baptist, the name of the church. The church is supposed to be the highest in the Peak District being 1,200 feet above sea level. The walk itself is along a fairly flat route, a gentle stroll around a high-level limestone village with fine views to be enjoyed.

The Church Inn

An interesting and welcoming one-room pub opposite the church. It opened as an alehouse in 1742 so they've certainly 'shifted some ale' since then. In the 18th century it was known as the Blacksmith's Arms. There are a couple of ghosts here – well, they did used to use the pub for inquests.

Marston's Bitter, Adnam's Southwold Bitter and Marston's Pedigree can be found at the bar plus guests like Cameron's Strongarm. Then there's Strongbow Dry Cider. There is also a wide variety of food and this appears to be popular as the pub is rarely without someone coming and going. So whether you prefer a light snack or something more substantial you should find something to appeal to you. The snacks include cheese and onion toasties, sandwiches and jacket potatoes, with main courses such as breaded plaice, breaded scampi, home-made chicken Kiev, and home-made lasagne. There are specials so you could expect to see dishes like beef and Guinness with new potatoes and vegetables on the blackboard. The pub is open from noon until 3 pm and 7 pm until 11 pm every day. Incidentally accommodation is also available here. Telephone: 01298 85319.

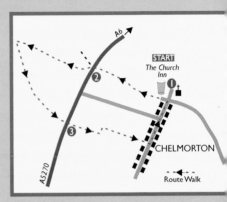

right fork proceeds into the farmyard. The old field system can be seen to your left. Keep on the gravel track. It forms part of the Midshires Way – a long distance footpath running for over 220 miles from the Ridgeway northwards.

② When you reach the road there are two tracks opposite. Take the one on the left (Caxterway Lane). Ahead are the higher parts of Buxton but you'll also see some of the unsightly quarries thereabouts. Ignore the first 'green lane' to the left but take the second one – about 150 yards before a tumbled-down stone building. Away to the right you'll get a glimpse of Back Dale. Proceed along the green lane but ignore another that forks right beyond a farm gate. Eventually you arrive back at the road.

PLACES OF INTEREST NEARBY

With **Buxton** and **Bakewell** nearby there is much to choose from. Alternatively if you would like to sight-see then **Millers Dale** and **Monsal Dale** to the north-east are worth considering as is **Tideswell** (and its 'Cathedral of the Peak') to the north.

The Walk

① From the Church Inn walk down the road for 50 yards. Opposite the road heading left, turn right along a gravel track. Stay on this, bearing left where the

The fields near Chelmorton

3 Cross this to the green lane opposite. This is rather more tree-lined than the others. Ignore the first green lane to the left. Shortly afterwards follow the lane round to the left. After 100 yards turn right over a stile into the field and walk down the right side. To your left is Chelmorton Low – a 'low' hereabouts being a high piece of ground! In the next field walk down the left side. Beyond this walk down the path beside the house, through the garden. Then walk down the drive to the road. Turn left at the road back to the pub.

Bakewell
The Peacock

MAP REF: OS OUTDOOR LEISURE 24 (GR 219686)	WALK 10	DISTANCE: 4 MILES

DIRECTIONS TO START: CROSS THE WYE ON THE A619 HEADING SOUTH INTO BAKEWELL. TAKE THE FIRST LEFT. THE PEACOCK IS ON YOUR LEFT ALMOST IMMEDIATELY. IF YOU COME FROM ANOTHER DIRECTION PARK FIRST. FIND THE PEAK PARK INFORMATION CENTRE. THE PEACOCK IS BEHIND **PARKING:** PARK IN THE PUB CAR PARK OR ONE OF THE PUBLIC CAR PARKS IN THE VICINITY.

Bakewell is probably best known throughout the world because of a tart which is in fact a pudding. The origin of the Bakewell Pudding is shrouded in confusion. Was it first made because someone added the wrong ingredient or was it an inspired piece of improvisation? Was it one family who first made it – or was it another? You will get conflicting answers if you ask these questions of any Bakewell resident. One thing is for sure – if you've got a sweet tooth you'll like Bakewell Pudding and one thing you'll learn (like so many things in life) is that there ain't nothing like the real thing. But what of the walk I hear you say. This is gorgeous Peak District scenery, the view towards Longstone Edge as you walk along the bridleway being possibly the pick of the bunch. The route follows the Monsal Trail, along an old railway line, and crosses the River Wye both going and on the return to the Peacock.

The Peacock

A popular pub which stands near to where the cattle market used to be. The market is now on the other side of the river. The pub was built in 1819 to house some of the 500 travellers who came through Bakewell every week. Inside are some interesting photographs of previous landlords and ladies. A resident female ghost, believed to be a relative of the first landlord, is friendly though she can get agitated when the present landlady is going away.

What of the pub? There's Timothy Taylor Landlord, Adnam's Best Bitter and Black Sheep available and Strongbow cider. When asked recently about his food, the landlord answered that they sell 'general pub food' which may in fact be underselling the pub. With dishes such as mozzarella lasagne and various steaks available you can see there is much to tempt you! No dogs are allowed inside but children are. It opens from 10.30 am until 11.30 pm every day. Telephone: 01629 813635.

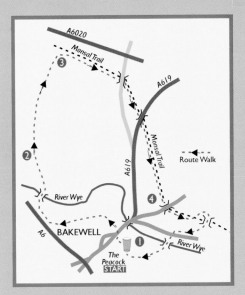

left and right). After 60 yards the path rises through the remains of various buildings. Stay on this partly concreted track to reach a farm gate with fields beyond.

② Pass through the gate. Follow the bridleway along the gravel track. Where it swings left towards the old quarry keep forward to the top corner of the field. Keep to the right of the dewpond to reach a walled track. Proceed up this. Longstone

The Walk

① With your back to the pub turn right to the main road. Turn right again. Cross the road to the Castle Inn, proceeding along Castle Street to the right of the pub. At the end bear left alongside the stream. Where this comes out under the road keep forward to the A6. Turn right passing Victoria Mill. After 200 yards turn right to cross Holme Bridge, an old packhorse bridge. Keep forward (ignoring the road to

PLACES OF INTEREST NEARBY

Besides the **Old House Museum** and **Chatsworth** (mentioned in the Longshaw stroll) there's also **Haddon Hall** (telephone: 01629 812855) along the A6 towards Matlock. A very impressive medieval building. In addition there's **Caudwell's Mill** (telephone: 01629 734374) a little further along the A6 at Rowsley. Here there's a working mill with craftshops.

The River Wye at Bakewell

Edge appears ahead. Enter an open field and walk down the right side. Keep on the bridleway to reach the Monsal Trail.

③ With Toll Bar Cottage 100 yards in front of you, turn right along the Trail for 1¹⁄₄ miles. This was the railway line that ran from Matlock, through the Peak District, up to Buxton. This provides a leisurely walk to Bakewell Station which was closed in 1967.

④ Stay on the Trail beyond Bakewell Station to pass under a bridge almost immediately. In ¹⁄₄ mile you reach another bridge. Don't pass under this – climb up the steps on the left. Turn right to cross the bridge. Follow the path down the left side of the field beyond to a driveway at the bottom of the field which takes you to a road. Turn right at the road. Immediately beyond Long Meadow House turn left into the car park with the Agricultural Centre in front of you. Follow the pavement round the right side of the car park to a footbridge. Cross this, then a second one over the River Wye. Upstream there will be ducks aplenty waiting to feed off titbits thrown by visitors. Keep forward for 30 yards from the bridge you've just crossed. Turn right to the Peacock.

Ashover
The Black Swan

MAP REF: OS EXPLORER 269 (GR 349632)	**WALK 11**	DISTANCE: $2\frac{1}{4}$ MILES

DIRECTIONS TO START: TAKE THE B6036 AT KELSTEDGE FROM THE A632 MATLOCK-CHESTERFIELD ROAD. STAY ON THIS INTO ASHOVER. TURN LEFT AT THE RED LION. ASCEND TOWARDS THE CHURCH BEARING RIGHT IN FRONT OF IT TO REACH THE BLACK SWAN. **PARKING:** FEEL FREE TO USE THE PUB CAR PARK OR USE THE VILLAGE HALL CAR PARK NEARBY.

Peak Practice used to be filmed in Ashover – but it's a few years since this ended. There's more to Ashover than *Peak Practice* though! The church is well worth a look and unlike so many nowadays it is usually open. Inside you will find a fine alabaster tomb to one Thomas Babington, and also a near-unique lead font. It is surprising that more lead fonts weren't produced hereabouts since Derbyshire was renowned for centuries for producing lead from the nearby hills. The view from the Fabrick, the highpoint of the walk (literally), is also worth enjoying. A viewpoint on this ridge will help you identify some of the features you will see assuming the weather is fair and clear.

The Black Swan

The Black Swan is an interesting pub with good food. Part of it used to be a garage for the local undertaker. Then there used to be a cottage next door which was an abattoir and butcher's. Not surprisingly it has a ghost, though so far it's not been seen by the current landlord. You can choose from four good beers, Black Sheep Best, Courage Directors, Greene King Abbot Ale and Tetley's Bitter. If you prefer cider there's Dry Blackthorn. The landlord describes their food as 'classic country cuisine' and I certainly wouldn't argue with that as dishes as varied as traditional roast dinner, chilli con carne and whole rainbow trout pan fried with almonds are available. All at a very reasonable price. Both dogs and children are allowed in the pub. On Friday and Saturday the pub opens from 11 am until 11 pm, and noon to 10.30 pm on Sunday. Monday to Thursday it's open from 11 am to 3 pm and from 6 pm to 11 pm. Telephone: 01246 591648.

The Walk

① Beyond the pub car park take the path on the left. Walk alongside the fence on your left. Ascend the walled path under two bridges. Climb some steps to reach a driveway. Turn left uphill for 50 yards. Ignore the small gate beyond the garage. Pass through the farm gate immediately beyond. Walk up the right side of two fields ahead. Towards the top of the second field pass through a gap in the wall. Turn left up some steps to reach the ridge. This is the Fabrick (pronounced Faybrick) and to the right is a viewpoint. The route turns left.

② The path to the left reaches a road. Turn left. Ignore a lane forking left downhill, to reach a small crossroads after 40 yards. Keep forward to descend gently. Ignore footpaths to left and right. Just round a sharp right-hand bend descend the footpath on your left. After 15 yards bear right to a stile. Proceed along the right side of the wood ahead to another stile. Descend to a stile in the middle of the wall at the bottom of the field by the gate.

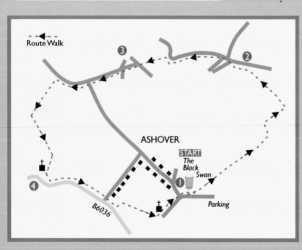

③ Cross to the road opposite passing Weavers Cottage. Descend the first road on the left. Ignore all left turns. The road swings right passing the Counting House on the left. At the crossroads cross over. In 100 yards beyond Marsh Green Cottage turn left into a field. Proceed towards the bottom left corner. However, after 175 yards pass through the stile on your left. Walk

Ashover seen from The Fabrick

diagonally across this second field. Pass through a gap into a third field and turn right, walking past the converted chapel to the road.

④ Turn left. In 60 yards beyond Narrowleys Road turn left on a path. Walk up the right side of the playing fields. Pass through a gap (ignoring a stile to your left). With the church ahead ascend the steps into the churchyard. Proceed to the church porch. Do enter if your boots are clean. Keeping the church on your left leave the churchyard to reach the Crispin Inn and read about the men of 'Asher' who left to fight at Agincourt in 1415. Keep forward back to the start.

PLACES OF INTEREST NEARBY

For those who like bird-watching **Ogston Reservoir** to the south-east is worth visiting. Remember to take your binoculars. Then there's Chesterfield which besides having the Crooked Spire also has a Museum and Art Gallery (telephone: 01246 345727).

Wingerworth
The Smithy Pond

MAP REF: OS EXPLORER 269 (GR 377667)

WALK 12

DISTANCE: $3\frac{1}{4}$ MILES

DIRECTIONS TO START: HEAD NORTH FROM KELSTEDGE ON THE A632. ONE MILE LATER TURN RIGHT AT THE CROSSROADS. PROCEED FOR 2 MILES. TURN RIGHT AT THE FIRST T-JUNCTION THEN A SECOND. THE SMITHY POND IS A SHORT DISTANCE ALONG ON THE LEFT.
PARKING: YOU CAN PARK IN THE PUB CAR PARK BUT LET THE LANDLORD KNOW FIRST.

A country stroll just a couple of miles from Chesterfield town centre. Starting from Smithy Pond – 'Smithy' was a person rather than an occupation apparently – the walk follows the main road southwards through Wingerworth for a while. You then head due south on an old track leading to the woods above Wingerworth. Walk up this track in spring or summer and tarry awhile at the ford. Flowers abound and it will be like stepping back in time, to a quieter less stressful world. What follows should maintain that feeling of wellbeing as you rise up to the highest point of the walk beside the wood to then walk along a lovely path through the trees at the top end of it. There's no need to rush – enjoy taking your time.

The Smithy Pond

The Smithy Pond is probably the newest pub in the book. It is very nicely positioned actually overlooking Smithy Pond, if you see what I mean. There's good fishing in the pond apparently, with Clay Cross Angling Club having the fishing rights. According to the last landlady this pond was owned by a man called Smith who was known as 'Smithy' rather than it having anything to do with a blacksmith or something similar. There is one thing about a new pub, it doesn't leave the landlord scratching his head when the history of the pub is asked about.

This is a very popular pub and it is easy to see why. It is nicely positioned and the food and drink are good. The beers are usually Tetley's and John Smith's. Strongbow and Woodpecker ciders are also available. As regards food there is a good choice with children being looked after with a menu entitled 'Foods Kids Love'. There are some interesting items like salmon and prawn pasta as well as the more usual fare like big burger stacks, grills and salads. Opening times are from 11 am to 11 pm every day except Sunday when the pub is open from noon until 10.30 pm. Telephone: 01246 557177.

The Walk

① From the Smithy Pond walk to the main road. Turn left. Ignore all roads off it.

A quarter of a mile later at Nether Moor Farm turn right. Keeping along the left side of the property walk forward to the green lane beyond. This descends to a ford (with bridge). Then ascend a delightful lane between hawthorn hedges. Continue uphill with Hardwick Wood a field away to the right.

② At a T-junction of tracks turn right towards the wood, but 25 yards before you reach it turn left into the field. Walk forward parallel to the trees on your right. When you reach a stile leading into the wood pass through this to descend to (and cross) a stream. Rise up the bank beyond before bearing left alongside a fence. This

PLACES OF INTEREST NEARBY

Chesterfield is just north of Wingerworth. See Walk 11 for the places to visit from there. To the east of Wingerworth is **Hardwick Hall** and **Stainsby Mill**. Call 01246 850430 for information on both these National Trust properties. Hardwick Hall (and gardens) would occupy you for an afternoon quite easily.

Walking through the wood

another two afterwards – walking between the fence and the wall in the third one. At the top of the third field turn right into the wood. Bear left (ignoring the path downhill to the right) and proceed along the main path until you reach a road.

③ Keep forward here ignoring a left turn. Stay on the road – a quiet country lane for ¹/₂ mile. This is typical English scenery with hedges, farms and greenery. Turn sharp right along the driveway to Bay Tree Farm. After 70 yards pass through the stile on the left. Walk down the right side of the field. In the next field head slightly left towards the double farm gates on the far side of the field. Turn right at the road. Get on to the left side of the road before the T-junction. Turn right here along Birkin Lane. Ignore the right turn for Hardwick Wood. At the next T-junction turn right again – then left back to the Smithy Pond.

brings you to another stile. Keep up the right side of the field you then enter and

Elmton
The Elm Tree Inn

MAP REF: OS EXPLORER 269 (GR 503734)	**WALK 13**	DISTANCE: 4 MILES

DIRECTIONS TO START: FOLLOW THE B6417 HEADING DUE SOUTH FROM CLOWNE. TWO MILES LATER URN LEFT AND FOLLOW THE LANE TO ELMTON. THE PUB IS ON THE RIGHT AFTER YOU PASS THE CHURCH.
PARKING: PLEASE PARK IN THE BOTTOM CAR PARK – THE ONE FURTHEST FROM THE ROAD.

Elmton, up in the north-eastern corner of Derbyshire, is not one of the more obvious places to go for a walk but bear with me. You'll be surprised what an enjoyable route this is. Elmton may be a bit off the beaten track (surely an advantage?) but take the time to find your way there. You'll find a lovely country pub with a warm welcome and good food and drink. The walk itself initially follows part of the Archaeological Way. Then a fascinating section passes through Markland Grips – a Derbyshire dale in all but name. The return route follows a 'mile's-worth' of ancient tracks. One of them (Border Lane) is still the parish boundary between Elmton and Clowne which means it is centuries old. Let your imagination run loose as you walk along it. Think what might have been coming round the next corner 50, 100 or 300 years ago.

The Elm Tree Inn

A very welcoming pub with a separate restaurant – the Barn Owl Restaurant. The Elm Tree Inn has been a pub or alehouse for over 400 years. Look out for the gargoyle built into the outside of the pub chimney on the furthest side from the road. It's hard to believe now but 150 years ago over 350 people used to live in this area, so that's why a pub like this survived before the advent of the motor car. The Barn Owl Restaurant is a converted barn. There's a good choice of beers with Old Speckled Hen, Wells' Bombardier, Adnams Broadside and both Tetley and Black Sheep bitters (plus a guest such as Skinners Cornish Blonde). Then there's Strongbow cider if you prefer. You will also find plenty to choose from on the menu with items of the 'All Day Pub Menu' such as sandwiches, nachos, jacket potatoes, salad bowls and burgers. The main courses include sirloin steak, mixed grill and chilli and rice. It gets better on the specials board where you might see chicken supreme and three-cheese pasta. The pub is open from 11.30 am until 11 pm though on Sunday it's noon until 10.30 pm – food is available in the bar from 11.30 am (Sunday from noon) until 9.30 pm. Telephone: 01909 721261.

Turn immediately left alongside a wall. Beyond this walk forward through the fields towards the road running directly away from you in the distance.

② Turn left at the road junction for a mile. About 250 yards beyond Hazelmere Farm, on a gentle right-hand bend, turn left along a narrow lane. Pass Upper Mill Farm. Immediately past the last building on the left, turn left alongside a high wall. At the end of the wall turn right. Follow the path up the wooded valley – Markland

PLACES OF INTEREST NEARBY

Cresswell Crags to the east of Elmton is a fascinating place. Telephone 01909 720378 for details. In Worksop (also to the east) is Mr Straw's House, a small semi-detached National Trust property as far removed from, say, Hardwick Hall as can be imagined. For details of opening times telephone 01909 482380.

The Walk

① With your back to the pub turn left along the road. Turn right at the church and 100 yards later (before the left-hand bend) turn right through the gateway.

The path near Upper Mill Farm

Grips, a 'grip' being a local word for a alley such as this. Where the path forks take the left fork to cross a concrete ridge over the stream. Turn left to pass through a short concrete tunnel. Beyond this turn right. Shortly afterwards ignore all paths forking right uphill. Keep forward until you are ten yards from the gravel bed of the old railway line. Turn left here by a concrete gatepost then immediately right towards the electricity pylon 60 yards ahead. Pass through onto the right side of the hedge. Bear left along the green lane between hedges passing below the pylon to your right.

3 Keep forward on this track towards Markland Farm ahead. Cross the stile by the gate in front of the farm. Proceed forward with the buildings to your left. Head towards a gap in the hedge 30 yards to the right of a concrete water trough. Keep in the same direction to the far corner of the field. Take care at the road junction. Stay in the same direction along Ridgeway.

4 After 40 yards bear left on the lane signed 'Except for Access'. This narrow lane runs along the edge of Clowne. At a grassy triangle ignore a path to the right alongside a stream. Proceed for 50 yards and fork left. Pass Grange Farm. Continue and, after ignoring a track to the right, keep forward to the road. Walk uphill back to Elmton.

Crowdecote
The Packhorse Inn

MAP REF: OS OUTDOOR LEISURE 24 (GR 101652)

WALK 14

DISTANCE: 2½ MILES

DIRECTIONS TO START: FROM THE A515 AT THE CROSSROADS WEST OF MONYASH TAKE THE ROAD HEADING WEST FOR LONGNOR. STAY ON THIS ROAD UNTIL IT ZIGZAGS STEEPLY DOWNHILL. THE PACKHORSE IS ON THE LEFT IN THE HAMLET OF CROWDECOTE. **PARKING:** IT IS ALL RIGHT TO USE THE PUB CAR PARK BUT LET THE LANDLORD KNOW FIRST PLEASE.

The walk starts at Crowdecote (pronounced 'Croudicot') which is *just* inside Derbyshire. After walking up the Derbyshire side of the River Dove you'll soon cross into Staffordshire at Beggars Bridge. As you get to this point (and probably for sometime before this) you'll have noticed the distinctive shapes of Chrome Hill and Parkhouse Hill further up the valley. (Whilst we're at it perhaps you ought to know that some locals call these hills, 'Croom' and 'Parkus'.) The only climb of the walk comes as you ascend the track up to the edge of Longnor. If you get the chance and have enough time Longnor is worth looking round (or better still come back after you've eaten at the Packhorse). After walking along the lane with more fine views, this time over the Dove into Derbyshire, you descend from Edgetop to cross the river before heading back to the pub. You'll see a few walkers possibly but not the throngs you'd get five or six miles downstream in Dovedale.

The Packhorse Inn

Not surprisingly the Packhorse Inn is on an old packhorse route and there's a fascinating résumé of the history of the pub on the restaurant wall. There are some charming photographs too showing a world that is long gone. They can trace their landlords back to 1723 when George Naden was the man behind the bar. Some of these packhorse routes date back to the Middle Ages so you can see that the river crossing here goes back centuries. Timothy Taylor Landlord, Everard's Mild and Leatherbritches Goldings are regularly available at the Packhorse and then there is the odd guest such as Leatherbritches Dovedale Ale. If you prefer cider then Stowford Press is on offer. Then there's the food. Though the famous Packhorse All Day Breakfast is no longer available there is plenty more to choose from including starters like carrot, coconut and coriander minestrone. Moving on to the main courses, game toureen sounds tempting but so do seafood pasta, braised guinea fowl and steak and ale pie. For the vegetarian there are a number of dished including falafel. The Packhorse is a perfectly positioned pub on the River Dove with excellent walks on all sides. Children and dogs are all welcome in this pub which opens from noon until 3 pm and then from 5.30 pm until 11 pm – the pub closes on a Monday though. Telephone: 01298 83618.

The Walk

① With your back to the inn turn right on the road then almost immediately left on another. After 100 yards take the track on the left for Glutton Bridge. Follow this as it bears right, walking through the farmyard of Meadow Farm. Keep the buildings on your left. Stay on the track beyond the farm. Where it enters an open field walk towards the far right corner and along the right side of the field beyond.

② This brings you to a stile (with a tarmac driveway a few yards ahead). Turn left here down the narrow field. Cross the wooden Beggar's Bridge over the infant River Dove. Keep in the same direction beyond and rise up the field ahead. Keep forward towards a building, part way up the bankside ahead. Bear left behind the building and rise up the track. This climbs quite steeply to Longnor. Turn left at the road as you reach the houses. Then at the main road which enters the village turn left again. (If you want to explore Longnor then turn right here.)

③ Continue for 300 yards along the main road after turning left. Then fork right along the Sheen road. Continue along here for $1/3$ mile enjoying the views to your left as you proceed. Opposite Edgetop on the right take the footpath on your left. This heads diagonally right downhill. Pass through the hawthorns to reach a wall. Turn left at this then almost immediately

PLACES OF INTEREST NEARBY

After your meal why not drive back to Longnor and have a walk round. You could visit **Heirs and Graces** at The Old Chapel. This is not just a haven for patchworkers and quilters but also a Doll's Hospital. Visitors are welcome, particularly sewing enthusiasts. For further information telephone 01298 83894.

Crowdecote

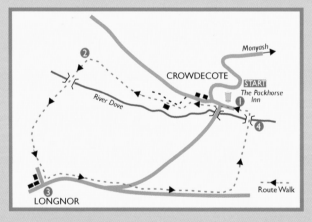

right. Walk down the left side of the field beyond. Keep forward in the same direction when the field opens out on your left.

④ Cross another bridge back over the Dove. Walk forward for 20 yards then turn left along the track which brings you back to Crowdecote and the Packhorse Inn.

Bolsover
The Anchor Inn

MAP REF: OS EXPLORER 269 (GR 474705)	WALK 15	DISTANCE: 3¼ MILES

DIRECTIONS TO START: ENTER BOLSOVER ON THE A632 FROM CHESTERFIELD TO THE EAST. TURN RIGHT OPPOSITE THE WHITE SWAN AND FOLLOW THE ROAD ROUND TO THE RIGHT.
PARKING: YOU CAN PARK IN THE SMALL CAR PARK BESIDE THE ANCHOR INN. ALTERNATIVELY USE ONE OF THE PUBLIC CAR PARKS NEARBY.

There will be cynics who will think this stroll is in the book to make up the thirty – a token nod to North East Derbyshire. Don't you believe it. This walk is in on merit. Towards the end of the walk as you ascend the fields below Bolsover Castle admire the impressive proportions of the 17th century castle above you. 'Tis said Charles I visited here. Of more recent vintage is New Bolsover, one of the earliest (if not *the* earliest) model villages, built for local colliers at the end of the 19th century. Two hundred houses make up the three sides surrounding a central green. The route passes through the model village. This walk is not all about architecture though. It also shows the excellent reclamation/restoration work being undertaken with EU funding. So take your binoculars and have a look at the Carr Vale Nature Reserve. This is a fascinating area.

The Anchor Inn

The Anchor Inn is the meeting place of the Bolsover and District Group of the Ramblers' Association so it is obviously approved of by local walkers. I'm sure you will like it too. Bella, a former landlady, is reckoned to haunt the place and indeed the current landlord has noticed a strange smell of tobacco when he's been down in the cellars. Dogs won't stop in the top bedroom and things have been known to move. So, watch out. It's obviously an old pub as there are 'ships' beams' in the attic. The beers on offer are John Smith's Extra Cold and John Smith's Smooth. Also, both Strongbow and Woodpecker cider are available.

Unfortunately, the Anchor Inn has stopped serving food recently. As an alternative, I would suggest you visit one of the other pubs in Bolsover. The Black Bull Inn, on Hill Top, comes highly recommended and serves some nice, if rather interesting, meals. You can expect to see ostrich, kangaroo and crocodile on the menu on their Exotic Game Night, as well as more traditional choices. The Black Bull Inn is open from 10 am daily. Telephone: 01246 822337 for more detailed opening hours.

The Anchor Inn opens all day from 11 am to 11 pm (except Sundays when it opens from noon until 10.30 pm). Telephone: 01246 241324.

The Walk

① Return to the A632. Follow it downhill from the town centre. Ignore Bolsover

PLACES OF INTEREST NEARBY

The obvious place to visit whilst in Bolsover is the castle. Telephone 01246 823349 for details of opening times. You may also wish to visit the remains of Sutton Scarsdale Hall (telephone: 01246 822844). Also consider buying a copy of the two Bolsover Trail leaflets which give more information about Bolsover.

Hill. Beyond, with steps on the right, take the gravel path on the left of the road. Walk below Bolsover Castle. Where the path turns sharp left after 150 yards, walk diagonally across the middle of the field ahead to the far right corner. Bear right down a track and proceed down the right side of the redbrick houses of New Bolsover. Turn left between Nos 21 and 23. Keep forward to the village green in the middle of this model village built in the 1890s for local miners. On the far side of the green turn right keeping the house on your left.

② Turn left at the road, keeping forward where it turns left. Keep forward at the crossroads of tracks. Follow the track as it bears right towards Carr Vale Flash. At the bottom pass through a gap in the fence on the right to reach an open area. Take the Stockley Trail as it rises ahead. Bear left at the T-junction to a viewpoint with information boards. Leave this along the track heading towards the M1. Ignore all paths to the left before swinging right. After 40 yards you reach the Peter Fidler Reserve (not signed at present). Bear right immediately along the gravel path. Follow this as it rises upwards then left. Proceed to reach another track. Turn right in the direction of the castle. Turn left through the car park at the top of the

Bolsover Castle

ise. Follow the access road towards the A632.

③ At the roundabout turn right on the left side of the road towards Bolsover. Beyond the Castle Arms turn right along Villas Road. Turn left into the field before the first house. Proceed alongside a hedge on the right. At the corner head towards the centre of the castle. Ascend the left side of the field below the castle. Immediately below it turn right. Bear left after 50 yards with the castle still to your left to follow a

tarmac path to reach a road. Follow this round to the left. Proceed along Castle Street past the school on the left. Bear right back to the start.

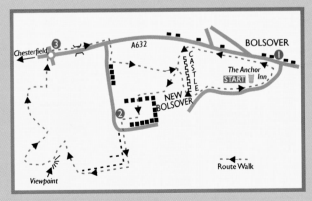

Biggin by Hartington
The Waterloo

MAP REF: OS OUTDOOR LEISURE 24 (GR 153595)

WALK 16

DISTANCE: 3 MILES

DIRECTIONS TO START: FROM THE JUNCTION OF THE A515 WITH THE A5012 AT NEWHAVEN HEAD SOUTH ON THE A515. HALF A MILE LATER TURN RIGHT FOR BIGGIN. THE PUB IS ON THE RIGHT AT THE WESTERN END OF THE VILLAGE. **PARKING:** YOU CAN PARK IN THE PUB CAR PARK WITH PERMISSION OR PARK ON THE ROAD NEAR THE CHURCH.

Just under half of this route follows the Tissington Trail as it swings in an arc around the eastern side of Biggin. This particular stretch gives you an ideal opportunity to view the hills of Dovedale away to your left. Indeed the original route of this walk would have had another half mile on the Tissington Trail – if the path through the fields hadn't been so convoluted. Ruby Wood is a good spot to have a break so take a drink with you for a short stop. You can learn about Muttley while you're there, the horse ridden by a former National Park Ranger on the Tissington Trail. Returning to Biggin you pass 17th century Biggin Hall, now a popular country house hotel. Incidentally, it's Biggin by Hartington because less than 10 miles away there's another Biggin – Biggin by Hulland.

The Waterloo

As I've mentioned before if the locals like a pub it's a good sign and it's obvious the locals certainly like the Waterloo. It's also frequented by walkers as well as visitors to the caravan site. The Waterloo has five darts teams and five dominoes teams. In addition they also organise karaoke nights and quiz evenings so it's a busy pub. Although there is no accommodation there is a caravan site behind it.

Black Sheep Best Bitter and Special Ale are on sale with guests such as Timothy Taylor Landlord. There's also Strongbow cider if you prefer. The food is varied and tasty with something for everyone. Whether you fancy a snack or something more substantial such as lamb hotpot and crusty bread, mixed grill or vegetable lasagne there is plenty to choose from. There is also a good range of coffees available too as well as tea and chocolate. Opening times are usually all day on Friday, Saturday and Sunday. On Monday they open from noon until 3.30 pm and from 6.30 pm until 11 pm, then on Tuesday, Wednesday and Thursday from 11 am until 3.30 pm and 6.30 pm until 11 pm. Telephone: 01298 84284.

The Walk

① From the Waterloo turn left up the road. Ignore the road to the right at the church. Turn left on the path 60 yards later (having ignored Percival Close). The path leads into fields behind the village.

Walk up the left side of the first one. Head diagonally across the second field to the top left corner. Keep on the right side of the third to pass through a wicket gate and bear right up to the Tissington Trail.

② Turn left on the Trail. A mile later you reach Ruby Wood planted to mark the Peak Park's 40th anniversary. Look out for the mole! The wood was planted in an enclosure named after the horse that was used by the local Ranger some years ago. Have a stop here, it is usually quiet and peaceful. Back on the Trail press on to pass under the road bridge.

③ After ¼ mile (just before another picnic area/car park) turn very sharp left off the Trail onto a path between walls.

PLACES OF INTEREST NEARBY

Head north-west to the **Old Cheese Shop**, Hartington (open 9 am until 4.30 pm every day). One of the few places where true Stilton can be made legally. Alternatively travel a few miles north on the A515 to **Parsley Hay** (telephone: 01298 84493). Hire a bike to ride on the Trail you've just walked on.

The Tissington Trail

This runs parallel to (but above) the Trail on your left for a short way. Keep on the left side of the fields beyond to reach a walled track. Follow this to White House Farm and a tarmac drive to the left. Follow this to the crossroads. Walk straight across and proceed along the main street of Heathcote. This eventually becomes a track which you should follow. Beyond the houses where the track bears left keep forward through the stile and cross the field to the stile opposite. In the second field head to the far left corner. Proceed on the right side of the third field. Then in the fourth field continue in the direction of the church tower, bearing slightly left away from the wall on your right. Climb over the stile in the corner of the field and keep forward (past a redundant squeezer stile on your right) to walk down the gravel driveway with various buildings on your right including 17th century Biggin Hall. At the road beyond turn left back to the Waterloo.

Matlock
The White Lion

MAP REF: OS OUTDOOR LEISURE 24 (GR 301586)	WALK 17	DISTANCE: 2½ MILES

DIRECTIONS TO START: FROM THE ROUNDABOUT IN THE MIDDLE OF MATLOCK TAKE THE A615 TOWARDS TANSLEY. HALF A MILE LATER AT THE CROSSROADS AT MATLOCK GREEN TURN RIGHT FOR STARKHOLMES. A MILE LATER THE WHITE LION IS ON THE LEFT. **PARKING:** PARK AT THE PUB WITH PERMISSION. IF CLOSED, PUT A NOTE THROUGH THE DOOR GIVING YOUR VEHICLE REGISTRATION NUMBER.

This is a fascinating winding route which skirts the River Derwent and then climbs high to give some breathtaking views. If you're not keen on heights then stay back from the edge as you proceed up to High Tor. BE WARNED – if you have children or dogs with you then keep a very close eye on them. There is a drop of a few hundred feet to the River Derwent below. Those with a head for heights might want to snatch a glimpse down into the valley, far below, though be prepared to see rock climbers ascending the hard way. Take your camera with you on this walk as there are a couple of fenced viewpoints where there are marvellous views of Artists Corner and St John's Chapel across the other side of the valley. There's also a very pleasant stretch of riverside walking before you start the steady climb up to High Tor.

The White Lion

It has quite a history does the White Lion. It used to be known as the Buddles Inn. 'Buddle' is a leadmining term meaning to 'wash lead ore in a trough'. The troughs used to be outside. It was also a coaching inn, being on the main London-York coaching route. In more recent times the author can remember playing darts at the White Lion back in the late 1960s on a Friday evening before going to the local disco! (Those were the days.) The regular beers are Marston's Pedigree and Riding Bitter with guests such as Hook Norton's Old Hooky on sale. If you're a cider fan then Strongbow will hopefully do the job. There are some tasty dishes on offer ranging from homemade soup to smoked salmon and an a la carte menu from Wednesday for the rest of the week. Opening times are from noon until 3 pm and 5 pm until midnight – Wednesday to Friday, noon until midnight on Saturdays and Noon until 11 pm on Sundays. On Monday and Tuesday the pub only opens from 5 pm until midnight. Telephone: 01629 582511.

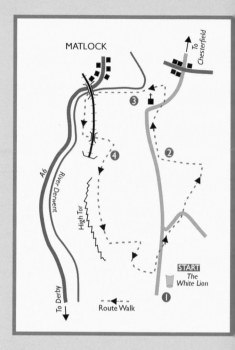

The Walk

① With your back to the White Lion turn right along the road. Beyond house number 162 take the low level path. At the end of the railings cross the road and ascend the steps. Proceed ahead to the road bend. Walk uphill for 150 yards. Keep forward off the road as it bends steeply right. Continue along the footpath eventually passing to the left of 'Falconcliffe'. Proceed on the path through the fields. Riber Castle looms above you. Turn left on a path running downhill from the right.

② Pass Highfields Lower School to reach Starkholmes Road. Turn right and walk downhill to St Giles' church. Beyond the lychgate bear left down cobbled Stoney Way. Some years ago a row of cottages was demolished here bringing part of the churchyard with them! At the bottom,

PLACES OF INTEREST NEARBY

A number of possibilities in complete contrast to each other. Firstly, there's the scenic **Heights of Abraham** with its cable car (telephone: 01629 582365), the model village of **Gulliver's Kingdom** for those who like rides (telephone: 01629 580540) and finally the **Peak District Mining Museum** (telephone: 01629 583834) for people fascinated by local leadmining history.

The view from High Tor

past Firbeck, turn left into the small park. Walk forward with Bentley Brook to your right to reach the River Derwent.

③ Follow the riverside path for some way with Pic Tor on your left. Pass under the railway bridge (ignoring a left fork before it). Continue forward with the Boathouse Inn across the river. After 120 yards pass under another bridge on your left. Walk up the path beyond, ignoring a path to the left after 40 yards. After 100 yards turn sharp right into the High Tor Grounds which were laid out in Victorian times.

④ Follow the path to the summit taking advantage of two fenced viewpoints overlooking the Derwent Valley below. At the summit bear right at the stone arch (with seat) to reach another viewpoint – without railings! High Tor is very popular with climbers. Ignore the path to Giddy Edge – take the path immediately to its left towards the mast. Keep to the right of this and descend to a tarmac access road. Follow this downwards until it levels out and you reach a gate leading onto an unmade road. Proceed for 100 yards. Turn sharp right down the footpath beside house No 13. Descend for 200 yards then turn left on a path across the level ground. Follow this uphill back to the pub.

Bonsall
The Barley Mow

MAP REF: OS OUTDOOR LEISURE 24
(GR 276580)

WALK 18

DISTANCE: $2^1/_2$ MILES

DIRECTIONS TO START: FROM CROMFORD FOLLOW THE A5012. A MILE LATER FORK RIGHT UPHILL INTO BONSALL. TAKE THE SECOND LEFT ($^1/_2$ MILE LATER) AT THE STONE FEATURE IN THE ROAD. THE BARLEY MOW IS UP THE DALE ON THE RIGHT. **PARKING:** THERE IS NO OBJECTION TO YOU PARKING IN THE PUB CAR PARK OPPOSITE THE PUB.

Enjoy a walk leaving the Barley Mow to head up the valley to reach Horsedale. Here Cromwell is supposed to have slaughtered scores of horses though whether this was to stop them falling into Royalist hands or because they were the horses of Royalist soldiers is not known. The route ascends fairly gently through the small fields with limestone walls which are so attractive in the spring and summer. Add to that the flora which abounds in this area and you have an appealing combination. Walk this route on a misty autumn morning though and it is a very different place with a certain mystery all of its own. You'll also see evidence of the leadmining that has taken place over the centuries. One field, at the furthest point of the walk, is full of the bumps and hollows where lead was mined. A word of warning. Don't go jumping up and down on top of these. The mineshafts are covered but now and again they cave in. So, stick to the paths.

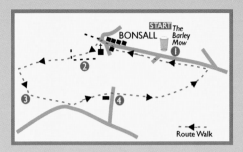

The Barley Mow

One of my 'regulars'. A marvellous, cosy, almost unique pub in my estimation. It is a fascinating place full of interest and particularly appealing with its open fire on a cold winter's day. It's excellent at any time if truth be told. The landlord is still leading walks on Bank Holiday Mondays and he's taken well over 3,500 visitors out into the Bonsall countryside. There is an excellent range of home-made food with my favourite being the cheese and onion pie. I know that the lamb casserole with stilton dumplings is very good as well as various other dishes such as scampi and tropical vegetable curry. Then there are snacks such as shepherd's pie, cauliflower cheese and beefburger in a cob. Don't forget the vegetarian and vegan menus too. The regular beer is Hartington Bitter but there are regular guest beers featured including Greene King's Abbot Ale. The only cider at the Barley Mow is bottled. Children are allowed but dogs have to stay outside. There are a few tables here which are very pleasant when the weather's good. At the weekend the pub is open all day (12 noon to 11 pm on Saturday and 12 noon to 10.30 pm on Sunday) whilst in the week they only open in the evenings from 6 pm until 11 pm. Telephone: 01629 825685.

The Walk

① Facing the pub turn left up the road. Past Flixons Croft there is a tumble-down building used in the past for spinning. Immediately after the cottage beyond the chapel dated 1893 turn left up the path, zigzagging up to a field. With your back to the stile keep forward up the path ahead. Pass through a gap in the wall. Keep in the same direction towards a small stone outbuilding. The path keeps to the left of this building to reach a walled track.

② Turn right up this track. Where it turns right keep straight forward (following the Limestone Way). From this track walk through four fields alongside a wall on your left, past another outbuilding in the first field. There is plenty of evidence of the lead mining that has taken place hereabouts. Please don't walk or jump on any of the bumps or hollows around here! In the fifth field after the track keep forward to pass through a stile into a sixth field. Immediately turn left. Walk beside the wall to a stile in the corner. This pockmarked field provides further evidence of lead mining.

PLACES OF INTEREST NEARBY
Besides those attractions at Matlock Bath (see the Matlock stroll details) there is much to see at Cromford. The **Masson Mill** complex includes a working textile museum (telephone: 01629 581001) and the 18th century **Arkwright Mill** was a cradle of the Industrial Revolution (telephone: 01629 823256).

An old stone squeeze stile

direction to a road. Turn left on the road for 15 yards, then left through a stile. Bear right to a gap in the hedge 20 yards away. Keep on the left side of two fields beyond towards Bonsall church. Keep in this direction, crossing a stile beside a gate with a track beyond. Initially walk down the track, subsequently keeping to the left of the buildings to reach the road.

④ Cross this, walking forward through four fields. In the fifth field bear half-left (towards the church). The path in the seventh field is very short, cutting a corner. In the field beyond keep forward for 40 yards then follow the wall round to the right, passing through a gap then walk alongside a hedge on your right to pass through a stile beyond. Zigzag downhill,

③ Cross the stile, walking diagonally across the field beyond. Crich Stand is visible 5 miles away. Continue in this first left, then right to reach a stile. Descend the steps to the road. Turn left back to the Barley Mow.

Tansley
The Tavern

DIRECTIONS TO START: TANSLEY IS 2 MILES EAST OF MATLOCK ON THE A615.
PARKING: THE TAVERN IS ON ONE SIDE OF THE ROAD WHILST THE CAR PARK IS ON THE OTHER.
YOU CAN USE THE PUB CAR PARK BUT ASK FIRST OR GIVE THEM A CALL.

This short stroll encompasses Tansley, Lea and Dethick. Three very different villages, or hamlet in Dethick's case. Tansley is where the walk starts before the stroll leads up to Cunnery Wood, 'cunnery' being a corruption of 'coney' meaning 'rabbit'. Look out for the 'gallows stone' which appears to be a discarded millstone. Still, it is positioned at a crossroads where often a gibbet would be erected and where suicides and ne'er-do-wells would be buried. *And* it is said that Dethick (down the lane) is a corruption of 'Death-oak'. Later on, the path all too fleetingly passes through Swinepark Wood before you reach Dethick itself. Here the Babbingtons lived in the time of Queen Elizabeth I. Anthony Babbington was involved in a plot to try and rescue Mary, Queen of Scots, who was imprisoned for some time at nearby Wingfield Manor. He failed and was executed as a result. A lovely walk packed full of interest.

The Tavern

Parts of this popular pub date back to the 1700s when it was a farmhouse. In more recent times it was the George and Dragon, changing to The Tavern in the late 1980s. The restaurant used to be a cowshed and reputedly it's haunted by an old milkmaid, Edith, who worked on the farm. The Tavern has had a good reputation for many years now and it is easy to see why. There is plenty of choice. Whether you prefer something simple and light such as baguettes with salad or fries or something more substantial such as bangers and mash or cod fillet there will be something to suit everyone. You could try liver and onions, Wingerworth pork loin, lemon and tarragon chicken, shoulder of Derbyshire lamb – you will have detected a local flavour to the meat by now. Nearly forgot the beers! There's a good trio available with Marston's Pedigree, Tetley's Bitter and Old Speckled Hen and for cider lovers there's Strongbow and Old Rosie Scrumpy. If you're wanting to stay in the area then perhaps I could mention that the Tavern has three B 'n' B rooms too. Finally, children are welcome when dining but dogs have to be kept outside. They open from noon until 3 pm and then from 6 pm until closing time in the week and on Saturday. On Sundays they open from noon until 11 pm. Telephone: 01629 57735.

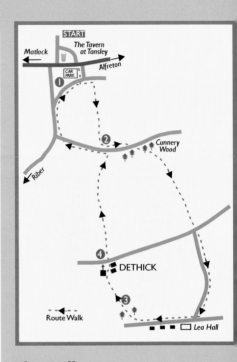

The Walk

① From the front of the Tavern cross the main road and walk up Thatchers Lane. At the T-junction turn left. Turn right 5 yards later up the path between houses. Then proceed to the top of the field. Keep forward to the stile in the top corner of the lawn. Walk up the right side of the field beyond. Pass through a stile. Continue up the right side of the next field.

② Turn left at the road to Cunnery Wood. Walk 100 yards alongside the wood before entering it. Walk forward then bear left to the wall on the far side. Proceed left alongside this. After 100 yards climb the stile on the right. Walk on the right side of the fields beyond to a gate. Continue along the track (Green Lane) beyond to the road. There are fine views of Crich Stand, Dethick, Bolehill (with its mast)

...thick church

...d Riber. Proceed forward (along Shaw ...ne) at the grass triangle after looking ...r the Gibbet Stone (an old millstone?) ...the grass to the left. At the end of Shaw ...ne turn right passing Lea Hall. Ignore a ...th to the left. Continue along the road ...Hawthorn Cottage on the right. After ...yards turn right down a delightful ...otpath signposted 'Tansley' and ...scend into Swinepark Wood before ...ing out of it.

...In the fields keep forward in the same ...ection to Dethick churchyard. There ...e no gravestones here but it is a hamlet ...eped in history. 'Dethick' was originally ...eath Oak'. Were hangings carried out ...re in the past? Pass to the right of the ...urch through the gate. Follow the path ...d bear left down the drive to the road.

④ Climb the stile opposite. Walk up the left side of the fields ahead. When you start to descend (with Matlock ahead) bear right to a bridleway then right to Cunnery Wood. Turn left on the road and return the way you came. Alternatively stay on the lane to a T-junction. Turn right down Alders Lane. Subsequently turn right down a narrower lane until you can turn left back to the start.

PLACES OF INTEREST NEARBY

One of the most popular attractions in the area is **Crich National Tramway Museum.** For further details call 01773 852565. Here you can enjoy a ride on the trams that used to be so popular in days gone by.

Brassington
The Miners Arms

| MAP REF: OS OUTDOOR LEISURE 24 (GR 231543) | WALK 20 | DISTANCE: 2½ MILES |

DIRECTIONS TO START: BRASSINGTON LIES 4 MILES WEST OF WIRKSWORTH. AS YOU ENTER BRASSINGTON FROM THE SOUTH FORK LEFT AS THE ROAD RISES UPHILL. THE MINERS ARMS IS ON YOU LEFT ALMOST IMMEDIATELY. **PARKING:** YOU CAN PARK IN THE PUB CAR PARK BUT PLEASE ASK PERMISSION FIRST.

The first time I ever saw Rainster Rocks they were bathed in sunshine with dark, menacing clouds behind. There was something almost primeval about them and I still regard them as a bit of a mystery, almost as though they don't belong here. The walk follows the same route that I used when I first saw them – walking up the Ballidon road as Rainster Rocks loom up ahead. This is a gentl introduction to the area around Brassingto (or 'Brasson' as it's known to some of th locals). There are good views and a chanc to see some of the old buildings of th village that would to a great extent in yea gone by have relied on the leadminin industry hereabouts (and agriculture course).

The Miners Arms

This is a traditional country pub, 250 years old and still serving the residents of Brassington, plus nowadays of course the many visitors to the village. The choice of beers covers Marston's Pedigree and Bitter as well as Banks's Bitter plus a guest, such as Bateman's XXXB. There is also Scrumpy Jack available. There's a wide range of good food to choose from too. Dishes such as Boozy beef casserole, Bhundi chicken curry and wholetail scampi may appeal to you. If you'd like something lighter then perhaps the bar baguette menu may be more to your liking and what about the 'Hot Selection'? The food is all homemade too. In short the Miners Arms prides itself on good home-cooked food including vegetarian. Since this book was originally published the landlord ahs changed and 'Guinness' the mynah bird has gone too – I never did find out what sex the bird was … Still, a change of landlord has brought some new ideas and I'm sure you'll enjoy a visit to the Miners. The pub opens in the week from noon until 3 pm and 6 pm until 11 pm. Then on Saturday from noon until 11 pm and on Sunday from noon until 10.30 pm. Telephone: 01629 540222.

The Walk

① With your back to the pub turn left uphill. Follow the road to the left below the church. Pass through the gate into the far end of the churchyard. Walk up the path with the wall on your left. At the lane

above the church turn left. Follow this as it winds through the top of the village ignoring all lanes etc to the left. After passing the new house on the site of the chapel dated 1852 you reach the main road. Turn right out of the village. After 400 yards turn right on the Ballidon road. Rainster Rocks soon appears ahead.

② Where the road turns left pass through the bridlegate to the right of two farm gates. Initially bear right on the grassy bridleway. Subsequently bear left through the ancient ridges and furrows. Rainster Rocks looms nearer to your left. Stay on the bridleway alongside a wall on the left. Shortly afterwards pass through a bridlegate. Continue in the same direction with the wall on your right. Pass into the next field towards a large stone barn. Away to the right is a redbrick 'lookout'.

③ Just beyond the barn pass through a gateway on the right. Cross the track. Keep forward through another gateway. Proceed alongside the wall on your right marking the enclosure around the barn. Stay beside this wall until two squeezer stiles (at either end of a short, narrow enclosure) are visible ahead. Pass through these. Continue in the same direction to

Rainster Rocks

the stile in the far corner of the smallish field ahead. Keeping in the same direction pass through a gap just below a clump of beech trees. Then bear slightly right along the grassy path through the hawthorns. Pass through another stile. Keep forward through two stiles at the top of a 'green lane'.

④ Keep forward under the electricity lines with Carsington Water visible ahead. At the far end of the field, pass through a stile taking the right fork almost immediately to reach the lane used earlier.

Turn left and follow it above the churchyard. Bear right downhill alongside the handrail. Turn right at the bottom back to the pub.

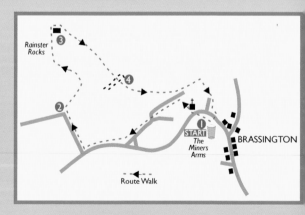

Wirksworth
The Black's Head

MAP REF: OS OUTDOOR LEISURE 24
(GR 286540)

WALK 21

DISTANCE: $2^3/_4$ MILES

DIRECTIONS TO START: ENTER WIRKSWORTH FROM THE NORTH ON THE B5036 FROM THE A6.
IN THE TOWN CENTRE IMMEDIATELY BEFORE THE ZEBRA CROSSING TURN RIGHT. THE BLACK'S
HEAD IS STRAIGHT AHEAD ON THE RIGHT. **PARKING:** THERE IS NO PUB CAR PARK. PARK
IN THE MARKET PLACE (IF NO MARKET) OR ONE OF THE OTHER CAR PARKS NEARBY.

This walk from Wirksworth Market Place leads up to the High Peak Trail via the National Stone Centre. Panoramic views from the Trail, towards Matlock, make the gentle pull up to it well worthwhile. On the way back a surprisingly rural stretch of path precedes the Old Lock Up and then the Moot Hall building. A figure of eight is achieved when you pass over the road which you used to leave Wirkworth. The final short, steep stretch down Greenhill highlights just a few of the fascinating and attractive buildings in the town. Afterwards perhaps you could get hold of a Town Trail leaflet and explore the rest of them. Wirksworth is full of surprises.

The Black's Head

At the top end of the market place, this is a good old fashioned pub though the food certainly can't be described as old fashioned, taking due account of visitors' changing requirements and tastes. It was built around 1700 and the early outbuildings included stabling and a piggery. It was previously known as The Blackamoor's Head. This redbrick pub looks attractive and intriguing from the outside and is a must for visitors to the town. Do try and have a look at the courtyard garden in the spring and summer. There is an extensive range of dishes such as homemade steak and ale pie, chicken and mushroom pie and steak and mushroom pie. There are large Yorkshire puddings, jacket potatoes and cobs. The beers are Hardy & Hansons Best Bitter and Olde Trippe with changing guests. Any child entering the pub must be 14 and accompanied. Dogs are allowed but not when food is being served. The Black's Head is open during the week from noon until 2 pm and from 5.30 pm until 11 pm. On Saturday this changes to 11 am until 1 am on Sunday and on Sundays from noon until 3 pm and from 7 pm until 1 am (ish) on Monday. Please note that meals are served at lunchtimes only. Telephone: 01629 823257.

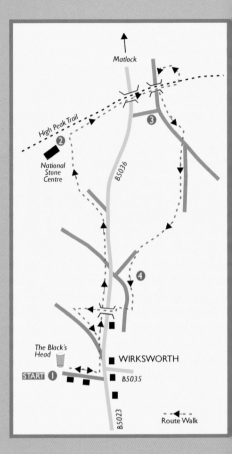

The Walk

① From the Black's Head walk downhill to the main road. Turn left towards Matlock. Stay on this for 500 yards ignoring all roads off it. Immediately beyond Cavendish Cottages bear left into Old Lane. Ignore all left turns. Ignore a path to the right. Where the track reaches a gate, fork right between three boulders into the trees before passing under a bridge. Keep forward beyond this to ascend through the

PLACES OF INTEREST NEARBY

The **National Stone Centre** has exhibitions and guided walks. **Wirksworth Heritage Centre** illustrates the town's history. In addition you may wish to go back and have a ride on the **Steeple Grange Light Railway**. Call Michael Strange on 01629 57759 for further information.

The Steeple Grange Light Railway

trees. Ignore all other paths to reach a path coming uphill from sharp left of you. Turn right here to a wide gravel track. Bear left uphill to the National Stone Centre.

② Beyond is a high, narrow bridge. Walk towards it but just before it, turn right uphill to the High Peak Trail. Turn right at the Trail for ¹/₂ mile. Pass the Steeple Grange Light Railway as you go. The Trail crosses above two roads. Fifty yards after the second one turn left down the path then left again at the road to pass under the Trail.

③ After 50 yards, at the junction follow the main road uphill. Some 200 yards after that bear right along Nan Gell's Hill. Ignore all roads off it. It then becomes Bolehill Road. With the Methodist church above to your left, turn right down the cul de sac past Bolehill Institute (1889). The route soon becomes a gravel track then a gravel path through a surprisingly rural area. Stay on this to reach a track which crosses a bridge. Rise uphill past the cemetery then a school.

④ At the road turn left for Whatstandwell passing the Old Lock Up. Fork right into Chapel Lane. After 100 yards pass the Moot Hall where the Barmote Court is held. This is a court which hears cases regarding lead mining. Immediately beyond the redbrick house next to the Moot Hall, turn right on the walled path. Follow this to cross the footbridge over the road. Beyond walk up a track and bear left into Greenhill. Descend this narrow attractive lane to reach the marketplace. Turn right and right again back to the pub.

Higham
The Greyhound

<table>
<tr><td>MAP REF: OS EXPLORER 269
(GR 391594)</td><td>WALK 22</td><td>DISTANCE: 2 MILES</td></tr>
</table>

DIRECTIONS TO START: AS YOU TRAVEL SOUTH FROM CHESTERFIELD AND CLAY CROSS ON THE A61(T) THE GREYHOUND IS ON YOUR LEFT AS YOU ENTER HIGHAM.
PARKING: THE LANDLORD HAS NO OBJECTION TO YOU PARKING IN THE PUB CAR PARK.

As you stroll along past the lovely honey-coloured houses of Higham bear in mind that thousands have already passed this way. You're following in their footsteps, footsteps that have paced this road for the best part of 2,000 years, if not longer. This, you see, is Ryknild Street, a Roman road running along the ridge on which Higham stands. As you proceed along the road an ancient market cross is passed. This used to be in the road and here farmers' wives would sell their wares and presumably farmers their produce as well. There is then a steady descent into the Amber valley where you walk past some fishing ponds before strolling alongside the river itself up to Ogston Bridge. From here a steady climb up an old track provides excellent views of the valley including Ogston Hall with Ogston Reservoir beyond. A varied and interesting walk largely known only to locals.

The Greyhound

A Wolverhampton & Dudley pub with a friendly atmosphere, good food and plenty of space. The Greyhound appears to be quite an old building which has been modernised, particularly inside. Like many pubs it seems to have a ghost or to be more accurate (and rather unusually) a pair. No one seems sure who they are though. Returning to matters less spooky: the food and drink. The beers you can choose from are Marston's Pedigree and Mansfield Smooth plus a guest such as Old Hooky. You have a very varied choice with dishes like steak, mushroom and horseradish pie, herby lamb, peppered pork, chicken mango with spinach and Moroccan tagine. There are also vegetarian meals such as cheesy cottage Wellington, aubergine stack and chilli lime peppers. Then there are fish dishes and pasta dishes and a great choice of desserts including apple and blackberry crumble, rhubarb crumble and chocolate chip brownie pudding. The pub is open from 11 am to 11 pm every day except Sunday when it's open from noon until 10.30 pm. Children are welcome and there's even a play area for them. It's guide dogs only though, I'm afraid, due to hygiene rules and regulations. Telephone: 01773 832016.

The Walk

① From the Greyhound turn left along the A61 towards Alfreton. Where this bears left keep forward along the Belper road.

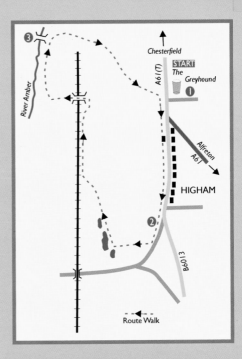

This takes you past a number of attractive buildings as you follow the ancient Roman Ryknild Street. Pass the market cross.

② Bear right down the Wessington road. After 200 yards (60 yards before the right-hand bend) enter the field on the right, through the gap in the hedge. Walk down the right side of this field and the one beyond towards the ponds in the valley. Cross the bridge at the bottom with a

PLACES OF INTEREST NEARBY

Hardwick Hall, home of the formidable Bess of Hardwick, and **Stainsby Mill** (both National Trust properties) are fairly near, to the north-east. Telephone: 01246 850430 for further information. Alternatively **Carnfield Hall** (telephone: 01773 520084) to the south-east is open by arrangement throughout the year. There's a Garden and Craft Centre there too.

Looking towards Ogston reservoir

pond to your left. Turn immediately right alongside a wood. Pass through a gate and proceed forward with a pond on your left and a brook on your right. Keep forward with a car park on your right. Follow the path ahead. 40 yards past the car park entrance, keep forward, ignoring a path forking left to a pond. This brings you to an open field. Keeping on the top side, proceed to the far end. Pass through a stile and continue with the railway to your left. Pass through a stile on your left, continuing in the same direction, between the railway line and a fence. Cross the footbridge over the railway line, the main line between Sheffield and Derby. Walk towards the wooden footbridge ahead. Before you reach it turn right through a stile to walk through the meadow ahead, keeping the River Amber to your left.

③ At the stone-built Ogston Bridge turn right up the track back to Higham and the Greyhound. As you climb higher a good view of Ogston Hall appears to your right.

Ashbourne
The Green Man and Black's Head Royal Hotel

MAP REF: OS EXPLORER 259 (GR 180467)	**WALK 23**	DISTANCE: 3¼ MILES

DIRECTIONS TO START: THE GREEN MAN IS IN THE MIDDLE OF ASHBOURNE WHICH HAS A ONE-WAY SYSTEM, SO IT IS DIFFICULT TO DESCRIBE HOW TO GET THERE BY CAR. IT CAN'T BE MISSED BECAUSE OF ITS 'GALLOWS' INN SIGN IN ST JOHN STREET. **PARKING:** THERE IS NO PUB CAR PARK. PARK IN THE SHAW CROFT CAR PARK (SIGNED) AND WALK TO THE CENTRE OF TOWN.

It's difficult to know where to start. Shovetide Football, the gallows-type inn sign of the Green Man, the Elizabethan buildings of the Queen Elizabeth Grammar School, Ashbourne Gingerbread, St Oswald's church and the southern end of the Tissington Trail. All add to the appeal of the popular market town of Ashbourne.

I'm forgetting the walk itself! This is a figure of eight with a difference. Why? Because a few hundred yards of the route is underground. So, where the inward route crosses the outward route (at least on paper) you'll be at a different level! This is due to the old tunnel at the southern end of the Trail (a former railway) being recently opened up thanks to the efforts of Sustrans. An excellent idea. All will be revealed when you undertake the walk, which introduces you to some of the delights of Ashbourne before heading out into the peaceful surrounding countryside, enjoying some good views, before returning along the Tissington Trail.

The Green Man and Black's Head Royal Hotel

There is insufficient space to cover everything there is to tell about this hotel here. It is a really excellent place – particularly the Boswell Bar which oozes tradition. It's oak panelled, has an open fire and is full of interesting artefacts including clocks showing the time in Paris, Moscow, New York, Tokyo, Sydney and, most important of all, the Boswell Bar. This bar is, of course, named after James Boswell who with Dr Samuel Johnson used to visit the Green Man in the 18th century. You can almost imagine them sitting either side of the open fire. (If you want something livelier than the Boswell Bar try the Johnson Bar.) Incidentally, the 'Royal' in the hotel name was added after Princess Victoria (as she then was) took tea here. I wonder if she was amused? There are Bass and Pedigree bitters available plus Strongbow cider. As regards food you have an interesting and mouth-watering choice. There are the traditional items such as jacket potatoes (with interesting fillings), grills and steaks, salad platters and fish and seafood. Then there are more unusual dishes such as sweet chilli chicken and mushroom and courgette linguine. I'm sure you will really like this hotel and do try the Boswell Bar if you can. The hotel is open from 11 am until 11 pm every day, though food is not served between 2.30 pm and 6 pm. Telephone: 01335 345783.

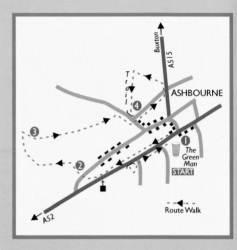

The Walk

① With your back to the Green Man turn left along the main street. Stay on this towards the spire of Ashbourne church. This takes you past some of the fine buildings of the town including the old Grammar School. Immediately beyond St Oswald's CE infants' school pass through a kissing gate. Walk diagonally left towards a gate.

② Cross the road beyond and walk up the right hand of two driveways. After a good 100 yards fork left along a path into the trees. In the first field walk parallel to the hedge on the left to a stile. Bear half-right in the second field passing by the corner

PLACES OF INTEREST NEARBY

One attraction nearby is the **Tissington Trail** which you will have walked along. From the Mapleton Road Hire Centre (telephone: 01335 343156) you can rent a bike that will take you north on the Trail. **Alton Towers** (telephone: 0990 204060) isn't far away but after a good meal at the Green Man, is it wise?

Enjoying the view over to Staffordshire

of a hedge to reach a gateway. The flat top of Thorpe Cloud should be visible to the right. Keep in the same direction along a grassy track towards a stile 10 yards to the right of a gate. Pass through another stile 15 yards ahead. From here turn right downhill towards the hedge corner jutting out into the field. When you're about two thirds of the way there turn right to pass through a stile 20 yards uphill from a gate on your right.

③ With your back to this stile head half-right towards the left side of the fencing on the hillside. Proceed into the far corner of this field. Continue along the top side of the next few fields (ignoring a path to the right as you go). Then continue forward on a hedged path to the road. Turn right up this. At the top turn left along North Avenue. Then turn left down the Buxton road for 60 yards. Take the footpath on the left. Walk down the left side of the fields to reach Bentley Brook. Cross this by the footbridge. Rise up to the Tissington Trail and turn left along it.

④ At the Cycle Hire Centre walk forward through the tunnel. After 375 yards, at the edge of a car park turn left up onto the road with the Beresford Arms Hotel to your right. Turn left along the road. Then right along Church Street back to the beginning.

Kniveton
The Ketch

MAP REF: OS OUTDOOR LEISURE 24 AND EXPLORER 259 (GR 197494)

WALK 24

DISTANCE: 3¹/₄ MILES

DIRECTIONS TO START: KNIVETON VILLAGE IS 3 MILES NORTH-EAST OF ASHBOURNE ON THE B5035. THE KETCH IS OUTSIDE KNIVETON. AS YOU TRAVEL FROM ASHBOURNE IT IS ON THE RIGHT. **PARKING:** FEEL FREE TO PARK IN THE PUB CAR PARK, PROVIDED YOU HAVE A MEAL AND A DRINK THERE AFTERWARDS.

There's one thing almost for certain on this walk through the folds of land to the north-east of Ashbourne and that is that you're unlikely to feel crowded. Initially the walk arcs around the western and southern sides of Kniveton before entering the village itself. By the side of the telephone box is a water pump which was working not so long ago – it may still do so. Then we leave Kniveton to head through the fields back to the Ketch. As you go, besides good views over towards Thorpe Cloud in Dovedale, you'll also see some of the 'Goodall Gates' in use hereabouts. These are self-closing metal gates which have been designed (and in most cases erected) by Robert Goodall from Kniveton. He has been tireless in his efforts over many years improving the paths in and around the village and the gates are certainly very effective.

The Ketch

This is a pub that has excellent food and a very attractive interior, well worth visiting. The pub was originally a farm, Ketchum Farm, which subsequently became Ketchum Inn before being renamed the Greyhound. In the late 1990s it was renamed the Ketch, returning to something like its original name. The Ketch is now a Wolverhampton & Dudley pub. Marston's Pedigree is available and there's usually a guest beer in summer. Strongbow cider is on offer too. Children can stay until 9 pm in certain areas but dogs are not allowed inside. Incidentally, there's a children's play area and some nice seating outside for those warm summer days. What of the food? Well, one look at the menu will leave you spoilt for choice. There are seven starters and three fish options; there are vegetarian options; there are sandwiches; there's a roast on Sundays; and don't forget the specials board on which you might expect to see lamb stew or a trio of pork and leek sausages. All in all, plenty to choose from. An excellent pub. You'll probably come back for more. It opens from 11.30 am until 3.30 pm and from 5.30 pm until 11 pm each day. Telephone: 01335 342341.

The Walk

① From the Ketch walk left along the road. Turn left again after 100 yards down a track opposite houses on the right. Follow this passing Hollyfields House on the left. Keep on the track to reach a farm on the right. Pass all the buildings to enter

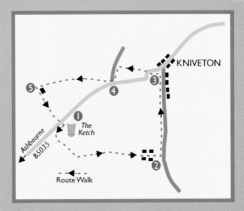

a field. Proceed on the grassy track. Turn left at the hedge corner. Walk downhill to a gate. Continue down the left side of the next field. Pass through another gate.

② Descend the track beyond, walking directly through the farm buildings. Pass a brick bungalow on the right to reach the lane. Ahead is Pethills – a tall three-storey farmhouse. Turn left along the lane. Over the wall to the right are remains of ancient fishponds. Keep on the lane through Kniveton to the main road. Look out for the old water pump beside the telephone box.

③ Turn left uphill. Where the road bends left proceed into the undergrowth by taking the path on the right side of the road. Keep on the right side of the ground beyond to reach a clearing 70 yards later.

PLACES OF INTEREST NEARBY

At Middleton Top to the north-east near Middleton-by-Wirksworth, you can hire a bike to ride on the High Peak Trail. Then there's **Carsington Water** (telephone: 01629 540696) where there are various craftshops as well as the chance to do some birdwatching from the public hides by the waterside.

The old pump, Kniveton

Ignore the track to the left. Bear right towards a smallish gate. Don't pass through it – walk along the path to the left of it. Pass through the 'Goodall Gate'. Proceed up the right side of the next three fields to Wood Lane. Turn left here.

④ At the T-junction pass through the stile on the right. Aim 40 yards to the left of the redbrick building across the field. In the second field keep in the same direction for a stile 200 yards away to the left of the electricity pole. In the third field walk to a small gate 50 yards from the far right corner. In the next field keep 40 yards from the far right corner. In the fifth field aim 30 yards from the far right corner! In the field with a redbrick farmhouse to your left, walk forward parallel to the field edge to your left.

⑤ Turn left along the narrow field. Go through a gate. Pass the garages on your left. Proceed along the drive past houses and another farm to reach the B5035. Turn right back to the Ketch.

Buckland Hollow
The Excavator

MAP REF: OS EXPLORER 269
(GR 375518)

WALK 25

DISTANCE: $3\frac{1}{2}$ MILES

DIRECTIONS TO START: BUCKLAND HOLLOW (NOT USUALLY SHOWN ON ROAD MAPS) LIES HALFWAY BETWEEN AMBERGATE AND RIPLEY ON THE A610. YOU CAN'T MISS THE EXCAVATOR. IT'S ON THE SOUTH SIDE OF THE ROAD. **PARKING:** PLEASE USE THE LARGE CAR PARK UNDER THE BRIDGE BEHIND THE PUB.

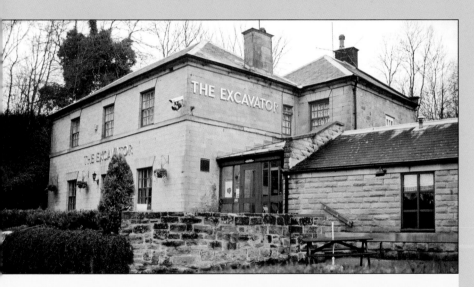

Buckland Hollow lies between Ambergate and Ripley on the A610. Someone once told me that from here as you travel north it is all excellent scenery, the start of the Pennines. Well, this walk doesn't go in that direction but it certainly has plenty of scenery and variety. The first mile runs along a section of the disused Cromford Canal although you won't realise it for the first $\frac{1}{4}$ mile. After climbing up to Pentrich (following a Roman road in the process) you have an opportunity to look round this interesting hilltop village. It spawned an insurrection in 1817, during the dark days of social unrest. Three of the ringleaders (Brandreth, Ludlam and Turner) were hanged and others jailed or transported. After leaving Pentrich you're back down beside the canal again on a wonderful stretch below the A38 which many people probably don't even know exists. It's tucked away between the banking of the road and a natural hillside. It can get a bit overgrown but this section is a real hidden gem.

The Excavator

This is a pub that opens 365 days a year and, although it seems hard to believe, actually used to have a real, life-size excavator parked on the roof. Well, it is called the Excavator. It was originally Ladybank House which was built in the 19th century. The wall inside the entrance is part of this original building. Ladybank House served as the canal house for commercial traffic on Cromford Canal. Yes, the canal used to run right past the Excavator though it is hard to imagine it nowadays. The property has also been an ice cream factory and a transport cafe. It's now settled down to being a very good pub.

Marston's Pedigree and Mansfield Smooth are both on sale as well as Strongbow. There is something for everyone on the menu with specials on the blackboard. There are vegetarian dishes such as vegetable lasagne. For the meat-lovers you can choose steaks, cottage pie, Cumberland sausage, steak and ale pie or maybe a double cheeseburger. All at reasonable prices. Incidentally, children are welcome but no dogs other than guide dogs. The opening times for food are Monday to Thursday 11.30 am until 9 pm; Friday it's noon until 9.30 pm; Saturday it's 12.30 pm until 9.30 pm and on Sunday from noon until 9 pm. Telephone: 01773 744400.

PLACES OF INTEREST NEARBY

The **Midland Railway Centre** at Butterley (telephone: 01773 570140) is just 2 miles to the east of Buckland Hollow. This is a great draw for steam enthusiasts in the area. In addition the **National Tramway Museum** at Crich (to the north-west) isn't far off either. Telephone: 01773 852565 for information about the trams.

afterwards ignore a right fork. Follow this to a pond. Proceed round the left side. Pass under the stone Starvehimvalley Bridge. Keep alongside the remains of the canal. Proceed beside the hedge in the field beyond. Bear slightly right across the field from the hedge corner. Keep in the same direction through the next two fields towards the redbrick houses. Walk along the front gardens of the properties on the left to the lane. Cross this. Follow the path opposite.

② Keep on the old towpath ahead. Eventually rise up to a road at the redbrick bridge. Turn left. After 130 yards turn right following a tarmac path across the field. Pass through a hedge to the A610. Cross (carefully) diagonally right. Follow the cobbled path up the bank and stay on it. The first section lies on Ryknild Street – a Roman road. Keep forward as the path becomes a track. At the farm our route turns right immediately past the last building. Before you take this path keep forward into Pentrich. Pentrich Historical Society has produced an excellent Revolution Trail leaflet which is well worth getting hold of, if you can.

③ Back on the route follow the path down the right side of the field with the A38 ahead. At the bottom turn right

The Walk

① Pass under the railway bridge behind the pub. Walk through the large car park and along the track beyond. Shortly

A disused section of the Cromford Canal

through a stile then immediately left on a track. After 130 yards follow this round to the right. With a large barn to your right keep on beside a netting fence, bearing left to a gate. Cross a stile and a brook. Turn left alongside the brook. After 200 yards turn sharp right to the canal. Walk alongside this for $1/4$ mile. What a delight.

④ When the canal disappears into a culvert climb the steps beyond, cross a stile then ascend 65 steps to the road. Turn right. After 400 yards cross the road and return on the

tarmac path you used before to cross the field.

⑤ At the road turn right. Later ignore the left turn at the George Inn to reach the A610. Turn left back to the Excavator.

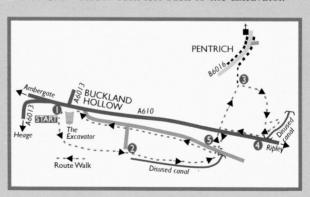

Doveridge
The Cavendish Arms

MAP REF: OS EXPLORER 259 (GR 117344)	**WALK 26**	DISTANCE: 3½ MILES

DIRECTIONS TO START: DOVERIDGE IS 2 MILES EAST OF UTTOXETER. TRAVELLING ALONG THE
A50 FROM DERBY FOLLOW THE 'DOVERIDGE' SIGNS IN THE VICINITY OF SUDBURY. KEEP
FORWARD AT THE ROUNDABOUT IN DOVERIDGE. THE PUB IS ON YOUR LEFT.
PARKING: THE PUB CAR PARK IS JUST BEHIND THE PUB AND IT'S OKAY TO PARK THERE.

A level walk in and around Doveridge in the southern Derbyshire Dales, this route follows a path which has been improved by Doveridge Parish Council and Doveridge Preservation Society. They have done excellent work for many years in the parish, opened up obstructed paths, built marvellous stiles and bridges and erected signposts with the number of the particular path on them. (You will see that the path you use to come back into the village is Doveridge Footpath No 1. Look out on the signpost at the furthest point of the walk.) There are one or two surprises on the walk such as the village pond and the old timber farm, Lower Street Farm. If you get the chance visit the churchyard and see the marvellous old yew tree. Then if you keep on down past the churchyard you'll find the impressive suspension bridge over the River Dove.

The Cavendish Arms

The Cavendish Arms is a solid old coaching inn which used to stand on the main road which passed through the village. Now the A50, which hasn't been built for that many years, has ensured that the traffic bypasses Doveridge. A mixed blessing perhaps. The pub is supposedly haunted but get in there on a cold winter's day, enjoy the open fire and any thoughts of ghoulish goings-on are likely to vanish fairly quickly – especially if you've got a pint in your hand.

Then you can start on the food. There's plenty of choice from steak and ale pie to baguettes (try the sausage and onion), jacket potatoes to specials such as chicken tikka masala and Thai red chicken curry. Opening times are Monday 5.30 pm until 11 pm; Tuesday, Wednesday and Thursday from noon until 2 pm and 5.30 pm until 11 pm; Friday and Saturday from noon until 11 pm and Sunday from noon until 10.30 pm. Telephone: 01889 563820.

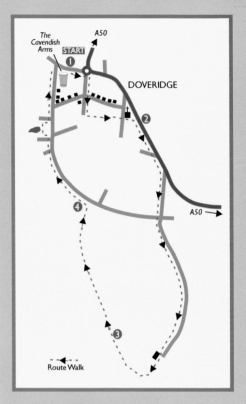

The Walk

① With your back to the front door of the pub turn right to the roundabout. Turn right down Sand Lane. At the crossroads proceed into Pump Lane. After 130 yards turn left along the path beside Cherry Hinton. Subsequently walk straight forward at the housing development, down the right side of house number 39. Proceed between fences and hedges. Turn right to Chapel Green, then right along the road for 30 yards. Turn left along a footpath. Walk on the left side of two fields to the main road.

② Turn right. Ignore Bell Lane. After 300 yards turn right into Yelt Lane. Descend to a crossroads keeping forward for $\frac{1}{2}$ mile along the cul-de-sac. Continue for 150 yards beyond some houses on the right. Cross the stile on the right, walking alongside the fence. Pass through a gate, crossing the stream. Proceed along the green lane ahead, and 80 yards before the end of this bear half-right towards the far corner of the field. As you go pass between two hedge corners jutting into the field on either side of you.

③ Cross the stile by the gate. Keep forward to the far right corner of the

The village pond, Doveridge

field ahead. Cross a plank bridge. Then head just to the right of the right-hand of two church spires. Beyond a pair of water troughs cross another, more substantial bridge. Turn left. Walk alongside a stream through three fields. In the fourth field bear slightly right. Climb the stile in the hedge. Cross the field ahead towards the stile to the left of a gate. Beyond it keep forward along the driveway to reach the house known as The Gables.

④ Turn left on the road, then left almost immediately. Pass timber-framed Lower Street Farm on your left. Leave Lower Street, continuing up Hall Lane. (This is the same road!) Continue up this road back to the start. There is an interesting diversion if you turn left into Church Lane, then right 70 yards later to reach the village pond.

PLACES OF INTEREST NEARBY

The National Trust property, **Sudbury Hall**, is just 2 or 3 miles east of Doveridge. It is a spectacular property and well worth visiting. In addition the **National Trust Museum of Childhood** is also based there. Call 01283 585305 for further information.

Duffield
The Bridge Inn

MAP REF: OS EXPLORER 259 (GR 351429)	WALK 27	DISTANCE: 3¼ MILES

DIRECTIONS TO START: TRAVELLING SOUTH ON THE A6 THROUGH DUFFIELD FORK LEFT JUST BEYOND THE DERBYSHIRE BUILDING SOCIETY BUILDING ON YOUR RIGHT. AFTER CROSSING THE RIVER TURN RIGHT IMMEDIATELY. THE PUB IS IMMEDIATELY ON YOUR RIGHT.
PARKING: YOU CAN PARK IN THE PUB CAR PARK BUT TRY AND GET THERE EARLY!

This stroll links Duffield with Little Eaton and gives you an opportunity to see something of a novelty – a pinfold incorporated into an allotment garden. A pinfold was a walled enclosure where stray animals were kept until the owner reclaimed them after paying a fine to have them released. The walk ascends and then descends the wooded hillside separating Duffield and Little Eaton. As you go you'll be following a section of the Midshires Way which crops up on at least one other walk in this book. Part of the Centenary Way created by the Derbyshire Footpaths Preservation Society is also followed (it coincides with the Midshires Way, at least on this walk). All in all, an enjoyable stroll (with a bit of a climb) in and around the Derwent Valley.

The Bridge Inn

This is a Wolverhampton and Dudley pub so you may imagine it is like a lot of others. Well, no. There's some very interesting food available, food 'with a difference'. So although you can go for the more traditional dishes such as rump and rib-eye steaks and lasagne, you may like to try something different like five bean burritos. Then there are some intriguing items on the vegetarian menu such as cheesy cottage bake and aubergine stack! So there is something to suit every palate. The beers are established favourites Marston's Pedigree and Mansfield Bitter as well as Strongbow cider. The pub was built in the 1930s and stands right beside the River Derwent. It is extremely popular so if you want to get a table it may be best to get there in good time. An early start to the walk and getting back just as it opens may be best! Enjoy your meal – I'm sure you will. Children are of course welcome. Dogs can only be allowed on the patio. The Bridge Inn opens Monday to Wednesday from 11 am until 11 pm; Thursday to Saturday from 11 am until 11.30 pm; and on Sunday from noon until 11 pm. Telephone: 01332 842959.

PLACES OF INTEREST NEARBY

Kedleston Hall (a National Trust property) is a few miles south-west of the start of this walk. Call 01332 842191 for details of opening times. In Duffield itself (by the A6) are the remains of **Duffield Castle**, another National Trust property.

tall chimney ahead. Follow the path through the wood, passing below the chimney, before rising to the road. Turn right on this for 250 yards with the Derwent to your right.

② Where the road bends down to the right, turn sharp left up the cobbled track. Ignore a path on the right after 40 yards. Continue for another 50 yards to turn sharp right on another path, rising as you go. A stone bridge over a narrow chasm leads to a field. Walk along the bottom of this field. Enter a wood. Ignoring a path sharp right, keep forward to a lane.

③ Turn left up the lane passing Heirons Wood, then The Hatherings. After 100 yards fork right on the footpath running along the back of the gardens of Little Eaton. When the path forks again, ignore the right fork this time. Keep forward at an access road. Pass a triangular walled garden, originally a 17th century pinfold, on your right. Bear left along the road (Alfreton Road) after passing the old pinfold.

The Walk

① With your back to the pub bear right up the road. Immediately turn right on the footpath with the pub car park over the hedge on your right. Proceed to walk on the left side of an open field, then a second field. Then enter a wood with a

④ Ignore all left turns for $^1/_2$ mile until you reach Whittaker Lane, part of the Midshires Way. Turn left up Whittaker Lane until it becomes a bridleway, climbing quite steeply up the edge of the wood to reach an open field on the left. Stay on the bridleway as it bears left

Looking towards the pinfold

through the woodland. Ignore a stile on the left and the path that crosses the bridleway at this point. After leaving the wood, keep forward along the left side of four fields. Leave the fourth field by a bridlegate subsequently ignoring a path to the left, and proceed forward descending steadily. This becomes steeper as you descend some steps. At the bottom of these turn left along the rough access road.

After 80 yards turn right downhill back to the Bridge Inn.

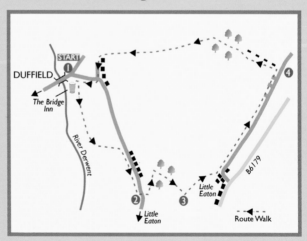

Church Broughton
The Holly Bush

MAP REF: OS EXPLORER 259 (GR 206337)	**WALK 28**	DISTANCE: $3\frac{1}{4}$ MILES

DIRECTIONS TO START: CHURCH BROUGHTON IS 7 MILES EAST OF UTTOXETER IN A NETWORK OF LANES DEFYING DESCRIPTION! THE VILLAGE IS MARKED ON MOST ROAD MAPS. THE PUB IS NEAR THE CHURCH WHICH STANDS ON THE NORTHERN SIDE OF THE VILLAGE. **PARKING:** IT IS FINE TO PARK IN THE PUB CAR PARK.

Another largely flat and non-taxing stroll through the countryside in southern Derbyshire. It passes through the grassy mounds of Barton Blount, all that remains of the medieval village that stood here centuries ago and which was possibly deserted due to the plague. Like so much the exact details are lost in the mists of time. The route then wheels around the buildings of Barton Hall.

There is a footpath to the church here though it is only an 'out and back' path. (If you look at your OS map you will see what I mean. It is worth having a walk down there if you get the chance.) Back on the route of the stroll, there is subsequently a good (though slightly distant) view of Barton Hall itself. After that the walk continues through the fields back to Church Broughton and a welcome drink at the Holly Bush.

The Holly Bush

The Holly Bush is a friendly village pub with quite a history. Inside there's a photograph taken in 1860 showing the thatched pub at the time. Coming nearer to modern times, during the Second World War airmen from Australia, New Zealand and Czechoslovakia were stationed at the airfield to the west of the village. Naturally the local English pub was a focal point for them when they were off duty. Some of the airmen have revisited the pub since the war although as the years pass their numbers have dwindled. There are also photographs of the various lifeboats built nearby.

The beers are Marston's Pedigree, Mansfield Smooth and Bank's Mild with guests such as Theakston's XB and Hook Norton's Old Hooky. On the menu are tasty items like steak and ale pie, freshly battered haddock – in fact the Holly Bush has fresh fish every week. So you may be able to sample monkfish or snapper. The emphasis is on fresh, local, seasonal food. During the week the Holly Bush is open from noon until 3 pm (except Mondays when they're closed) and in the evening from 6 pm until 11 pm (except Sundays when they're open from 7 pm until 10.30 pm). Telephone: 01283 585345.

The Walk

① With your back to the pub turn right on the road, then right along Chapel Lane. Cross the stile at the end of the lane. Turn left. (Ignore the signpost! Head for the gateway to the left of the willow trees.) Proceed towards the redbrick property across the fields. Then cross a stile at the far side of the second field. Beyond this aim for the narrow gap in the hedge on the far side of the third field, to the left of the white house. Keep in the same direction across the fourth field.

② Turn right along the lane passing some cottages. After 250 yards turn right along a track/bridleway. Stay on this to walk beside a hedge on your left. Continue in the second field. In the trees half right is Barton Hall. At the beginning of the third field leave the grassy track as it swings

PLACES OF INTEREST NEARBY

Kedleston Hall (National Trust) is to the north-east. A stunning building built for the Curzon family. Call 01332 842191 for details of opening times. In Derby, amongst other places, you could visit **Royal Crown Derby** (01332 712841) or the Industrial Museum at the **Silk Mill** (01332 255308).

Barton Hall

right. Keep forward in the same direction as before across the rough ground. Pass through the metal gate. Follow a 'hollow-way' through the field ahead.

③ At the hedge on the far side turn right (staying in the field). Pass through a gate. The uneven ground is all that remains of the medieval village of Barton Blount. Continue on the left side of the field. Pass through another gate in the corner. Head slightly left across the large field ahead of you. At the far side turn right along the track (still in the same field). Pass through a gap continuing down the left side of the next field. Keep to the left of

the wood. Cross a stile beyond it. Keep forward to a squat concrete building. Climb a stile just beyond this. With your back to this stile aim towards a stile in the trees slightly right ahead. Cross the driveway.

④ On the far side keep forward passing through the copse ahead. Beyond this head half-right towards the church. Keep to the right of the hedge corner walking towards the church. Pass through a gate. Cross the field towards the church. This brings you back to Chapel Lane. Return to the start.

Swarkestone
The Crewe and Harpur Arms

MAP REF: OS EXPLORER 245 (GR 369286)	WALK 29	DISTANCE: 2 MILES

DIRECTIONS TO START: TAKE THE A514 SOUTH FROM DERBY. THE CREWE AND HARPUR ARMS IS ON THE RIGHT AFTER A SHARP LEFT-HAND BEND JUST BEFORE THE TRENT. **PARKING:** YOU CAN PARK IN THE PUB CAR PARK.

One of my long term aims is to walk the length of the Trent and Mersey Canal from Shardlow in Derbyshire to Preston Brook in Cheshire, a distance of 92 miles. For the time being I've happily settled for this level walk from Swarkestone – a taste of what to expect in the future perhaps. As you walk along the canal there is, invariably, something happening, whether it's a narrow boat cruising by or the flash of a kingfisher flying just above the level of the water.

There are a couple of other fascinating features about this walk though. One is the Swarkestone Pavilion. This appears to have been a lodge where the ladyfolk could watch their men playing games on the green below. Then there is the cairn in the garden between the Crewe and Harpur Arms and the Trent. This marks the spot where Bonnie Prince Charlie turned back in 1745, the southernmost point he reached in his efforts to claim the throne.

The Crewe and Harpur Arms

A very attractive red-brick pub built beside the River Trent. You can't miss it. It's large on the inside, another Wolverhampton and Dudley pub. The Harpur-Crewe family after whom it is named lived at Calke Abbey not so far away. The food available is varied and popular. On the main menu are dishes like Thai chicken penang, Spanish chicken, Portobello beef, chicken mango with spinach. Then there are fish dishes such as Old English fish pie or battered haddock. There are specials such as duck breast, minted lamb hotpot and cod and prawn crumble. What about desserts? Well if you can get this far why not try rhubarb crumble or carrot cake pudding or perhaps chocolate chip brownie pudding. The beers include Marston's Pedigree and Banks's Bitter. The pub opens from 11 am to 11 pm every day except Sunday when shorter hours (from noon to 10.30 pm) are in force. Children are welcome, indeed there's both a play area and a menu especially for them. Telephone: 01332 700641.

The Walk

① Stand in front of the pub facing the river. Turn left and cross the road (the A514). Walk along the path bearing left after just ten yards alongside the wall on your left. This cuts through one or two gardens but soon comes out into some open fields. Stay on the right side of these until you catch sight of the church ahead. Walk forward towards this through the farmyard to reach the church gate. Don't enter the churchyard though. Turn left, keeping the wall on your right, to reach a grassed area at the back of the church. In the corner is a stile. Pass through this.

② To visit the 'bowling green' and pavilion stand with your back to the church and turn right along the wall side. At the wall corner keep forward to come out on a track beside the entrance to the Tithe Barn. Proceed forward across the track to get a glimpse of this unique structure. To follow the rest of the wall return across the field to the stile behind the church. Then with your back to the church walk across the field to a gateway through which a track reaches the road beyond.

③ Turn right at the road for 200 yards then right down the path to the Trent and Mersey Canal. Turn left alongside this to walk with it on your right for the next ^{3}/ mile. As you go you'll pass under a railway bridge before passing to the left of Swarkestone Lock. Just beyond Swarkestone Stop look out for the milepost indicating that Shardlow is 6 miles behind you and Preston Brook 86 miles ahead!

Swarkestone Pavilion

④ Continue to a lane that passes over Lowes Bridge (numbered 15 on the far side). Turn left along the lane to reach a crossroads at the edge of Swarkestone. Keep forward to enter the village along Woodshop Lane. Follow the road round to the left to reach the Crewe and Harpur Arms.

PLACES OF INTEREST NEARBY

Though Derby lies to the north the attractions suggested are to the south. Firstly, **Calke Abbey**, the National Trust property near Ticknall (telephone: 01332 863822). This is the sort of place that you will want to visit time and again. Then **Melbourne Hall** isn't so far away. Telephone: 01332 862502 for further information.

Rosliston
The Plough

| MAP REF: OS EXPLORER 245 (GR 246165) | WALK 30 | DISTANCE: 2¼ MILES |

DIRECTIONS TO START: FOLLOW THE A38 SOUTH-WEST FROM BURTON. LEAVE THIS, HEADING EASTWARDS TO WALTON ON TRENT. THEN FOLLOW THE SIGNS FOR ROSLISTON. AT THE T-JUNCTION AT THE EDGE OF ROSLISTON TURN RIGHT. THE PLOUGH IS ON THE RIGHT AT THE FAR END. **PARKING:** USE THE CAR PARK IN FRONT OF THE PUB OR THE ONE AT THE REAR.

Rosliston prides itself on its success with its flowers and gardens in spring and summer so you may wish to save this walk for that time of year, or perhaps return then if you're doing this walk in the autumn or winter. The village is in the heart of the National Forest – 200 square miles which are being planted to create a forest which probably won't be at its best for a few more years yet. Still, in the meantime it's good to see what they have achieved. This is a flattish walk with only the odd slope to negotiate.

The Plough

The most southerly pub in the book but well worth searching out. This is a friendly pub in an attractive village. Both Marston's Pedigree and Marston's Smooth are on offer as well as Guinness. Not everyone likes bitter of course so Strongbow is available on draught. There is a good choice of tasty food available with battered cod, wholetail scampi, gammon with egg or pineapple on the menu plus the Plough's Special Big Breakfast. Then there are specials such as madras curry with chips or rice. There's also a Sunday carvery.

It opens every day from 4.30 pm until 11 pm though on a Saturday they're open all day from noon until 11 pm and on Sunday from noon until 10.30 pm. There's a garden behind the pub and here in the summertime 'as and when' they feel like it there could be a barbeque. Telephone: 01283 761354.

The Walk

① With your back to the Plough turn left for 70 yards. Turn right on the path signed 'Caldwell'. Follow the track beyond for ¼ mile into the countryside. Where the track bends left keep forward along the wide grassy path, towards the buildings of Caldwell. After 400 yards (before the end of the wood on your left) turn sharp left over a stile into the trees. Follow this path to reach another wide grassy path beyond. Turn left for a few yards. Ignore the large gap in the hedge on your right. Walk past this and, a few yards later, pass through a smaller gap into the field. Cross this field heading for the solitary oak tree on the far

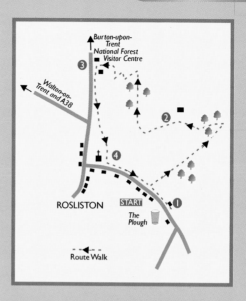

side. As you go keep Calves Croft Farm to your right. Cross the farm driveway to pass through a gap in the hedge to the left of the tree you were aiming for.

② Walk down the left side of the field ahead. At the bottom walk right then left. Cross a stile, then bear right before turning left over a small watercourse. Beyond this turn right on a narrower gravel path. Stay on this to reach a small fenced pond on the right. Turn left just past this on a gravel path to a hide. From here zigzag up the slope to the Visitor Centre (passing an analemmatic sundial as you go!).

PLACES OF INTEREST NEARBY

For an opportunity to see how beer is made why not visit the **Bass Museum** in Burton? Call them on 01283 511000 to see when they're open. Then if you want to learn more about the **National Forest Visitor Centre** at Moira contact them on 01283 216633.

The unlikely looking characters near the National Forest Visitor Centre

③ Pass through these buildings and under the striking wooden entrance. Keep to the left of the car park, heading for the road. Just before you reach it turn left along the path signed 'Memorial Plot Rosliston Village'. The lane is just over the hedge on your right as you follow this path. Ignore any tracks or paths to the left. Cross the field in front of the village aiming to the left of the church. Follow the path down the left side of the churchyard.

④ Having passed The White Cottage turn left at the road. Rosliston does very well in the 'East Midlands in Bloom' and 'The Best Kept Village in Derbyshire' competitions. In summer the flowers are a delight. Continue along the road back to the Plough.